MYSTIC TRAVELERS

IMAGES FROM THE EDGE

A TRAVELOGUE–MEMOIR BY

GAIL CRANE

First edition.

ISBN (print): 978-0-9915449-8-1
ISBN (e-book): 978-0-9915449-9-8

Design & Publishing by Rockin' Dog Studio, LLC, in consultation with John Edwards.
All photos by Jon Crane unless otherwise noted.

Contact: Gail Crane
PO Box 1100, Hill City, SD 57745
mystictravelers@icloud.com
Travelogue website: mystictravelers.us

To our grandsons—Calvin, Farley, and Dylan Crane,
and Miller ("Memo" to me) James.

CONTENTS

mystic travelers

INTRODUCTION

My husband and I are Mystic travelers—"Mystic" because our home lies far out on the edge of what most would call civilization, a pinpoint on the South Dakota map called Mystic; "travelers" because for work or pure pleasure, we go to places that are remote and beautiful, seeking newness, adventure, and inspiration. Teetering on the edge of distant and unknown places is a style of living that comes naturally to Jon Crane, but for me it has been an acquired taste. Through our life together, Jon's goal has been to live down a gravel road with no neighbors in sight, a place where the natural world of trees, rivers, and cliffs makes up life's essence. As an artist and a dreamer, he can thrive in isolation.

Dreams sprout, blossom, and can be shared in Mystic. A settlement of four year-round residents and a few summer homes, the Mystic Valley is tucked away between Hill City and Rochford, at the confluence of Castle Creek and Rapid Creek. Friends often arrive at our front door for the first time with wide eyes, wondering if they are at the end of the earth. Wildlife roams free. Ghosts of the valley's past hover over old placer mines, abandoned railroad beds, and remnants of stone foundations, humming through the ancient trees. Instead of the roar of a highway, we hear the happy chatter of bikers and hikers enjoying the solitude of a nearby trail. We are even removed from the din of television, keeping far from the edge of that ocean of noise and distraction.

In the beginning of our marriage, life at Mystic was a bit too far out for me. When we settled into our home, I tried to do what any city girl would do: install draperies. Jon looked at me with a questioning twinkle in his eye and asked who I thought might be peeking in. I laughed, knowing that the only eyes that might be outside our windows would belong to deer, mountain lions, or big horn sheep. But still, the habit of wanting to pull the drapes at dusk was difficult to overcome. Seeing the fierce blackness of night out the window required a big shift in my mindset.

For Jon, the edge is not a dangerous place. In his life, the blinds are always open to the world beyond. As a young boy, he loved nothing better than to spend the night in a tent in his own backyard in New Jersey, sleeping in the closest thing to wilderness he could find. He hiked the trails of the East Coast and fished the lakes and streams with his grandfather. His college years in Colorado were packed with camping expeditions into the vastness of the Rocky Mountain wilderness. As he got older, his adventurous spirit kept pace with the rigors of being an Air Force pilot, flying KC-135s during the years of the Vietnam War.

Meanwhile, in the flats of West Texas, I slept in tents in an organized Girl Scout campground, attended church regularly, and traveled throughout America on well-planned summer vacations. My parents saved their money for two purposes—education and travel. They wanted to open up the world beyond the horizons of Midland, Texas, to me and to my brothers. My mom was a master organizer, and even in our family camping experiences, nothing was risky or left to chance. At the University of Texas in Austin, I lived in a safe, all-girls dormitory while getting a degree in Education with minors in English and Spanish.

After leaving the Air Force in 1975, Jon picked up a paintbrush and began painting his way toward a future as a self-published artist. His fine arts degree from the University of Northern Colorado reminded him of his passion for painting but did little to prepare him for the trials of making a living as an artist. One of his toughest challenges was learning how to market what he created, so he hit the road in search of his audience. Road trips led him to art festivals around the country, and as he traveled, the quest for an audience also became a hunt for subjects to paint. Traveling from Rapid City, South Dakota, to shows on the Penn State campus, he explored the back roads of the Amish countryside, where he collected compelling images of remote farms. Shows in Texas and Oklahoma drew him south through a maze of secondary roads speckled with landscapes of the heart of America's farmland. In his own backyard, he investigated the inaccessible forest roads and the more distant out-of-the-way prairie lands, finding ancient structures and vehicles to fuel his creativity.

Jon was married, had a son, ran a gallery and frame shop in Rapid City, South Dakota, and continued to explore the heartland and wild lands of America. I married, had a daughter and a son, and focused on life in the city. My degree in education led me into public school teaching in Arlington, Texas. Life outside the classroom pulsed with interaction with other soccer moms, gymnastic coaches, Sunday school teachers, and my former husband's business associates. I followed paved city streets to a tidy house packed in solidly with other tidy houses. I never dreamed of isolation or tiptoeing along the brink of any precipice.

In the 1980s, our worlds shifted, as if two giant hands twisted the ends of our kaleidoscopes. We both divorced, we both moved, and in the aftermath, Jon and I became acquainted. I realized that a love for the outdoors and a desire to travel were two passions we shared. Still, those early years that grounded me in outdoor living and well-planned travel did not change my temperament. By nature, I have always been cautious, not one to push the limits or explore extreme edges of my world. After meeting Jon and spending time with this intrepid man, I realized I was going to have to change my style, or at least learn to cope with his. The second half of my adult life, which I have spent with Jon, has been an exercise in doing just that—leaning out, dreaming large, and reaching beyond the safe interior of my eight-to-five world.

One of my practice sets in adventurous living came early in our relationship, when we explored the Great Sand Dunes National Park in Colorado. Halfway through our climb up a dune, we spotted lightning on the horizon, moving our way. True to my prudent nature, I called for a retreat. Jon insisted on continuing. I plunked down in the sand midway up and assured him I would be right there when he returned. Lightning did not strike him that day, and as we scampered back down the sand amidst the beginning splatters of rain, he held my hand hard and shouted into the storm, "Take your energy from the wind and the lightning, Gail. Don't be afraid of the forces of nature."

Gradually we have learned to find our balance. Jon discovered that my heart for adventure has closer and softer edges. Patiently he discovered how to encourage me forward beyond my natural limits, conquering my fear with his vision and confidence. When the road seems too scary or the trail too steep, he holds out his hand and reassures me. He takes the lead as we cross over foreign borders, plunge into deep waters, or hike even higher for the most spectacular views. I have learned to trust him to keep me safe.

On the other side of that teeter-totter, my energy goes into navigating the social and business demands inevitable in real life. His creativity is derailed by phone calls, marketing decisions, balancing the checkbook and "doing lunch"—all a part of my natural habitat. I throw my weight into what, for him, are distractions, tugging him to that edge when he needs to be there and shielding him when he does not.

Through the twenty-seven years we have been married, we have found an extra joy in discovering God along the edges. We are such different seekers, and these discoveries come to us in distinct ways that reveal our differences. As a pragmatist, Jon encounters the Divine by immersing in nature, by seeking and reflecting the beauty of creation, being uncompromising in his understanding of what is True. I seek God in the company of other believers, in the of scripture, or in the great silences of centering prayer. With Jon guiding the way, I also have discovered Divine Presence in the heart-stopping beauty of wilderness and in the solitude of remote living. I cannot say our spiritual journeys are the same. I cannot say we have not had long and passionate discussions, each trying to convince the other of our convictions. But I can say our mutual respect for each other keeps us in the tension. In our own individual ways, we are contemplatives, open to the great adventures of discovering and embracing the Sacred in the journey.

Rainer Maria Rilke aptly describes what I see our relationship to be. "True love consists of this, that two solitudes protect and border and salute each other." This is what we do as we move in tandem through life. I invite you to come along with us as we share our haven, our travel adventures, and our soul journeys that stretch us, saluting each other, as we contemplate the magic and mystery along the edge.

For an additional library of photos related to our travels, please visit *mystictravelers.us*.

images of mystic

OUR JOURNEY BEGINS

chapter one

The West Texas day was blustery and unpredictable—just like my relationship with the artist I was flying to meet—but the early morning dawn of departure was infused with the color of hope. This was my second attempt to marry Jon Crane. Originally, we had planned to be married at a small private ceremony in Midland, Texas. We had settled on the venue and had even ordered the invitations when the groom-to-be suffered a serious case of cold feet. He called off the wedding. My girlfriends and I dressed in black, observed a wake, burned the wedding invitation proof—and buried the ashes in a backyard grave, along with my dreams. Within a few months, Jon's feet returned to normal and brought him back to me to try again. The wounded side of me said, "No, I would never plan another wedding." The wholly in-love part of me said, "Yes, we can try again," as long as he made it happen. Frankly, I did not hold my breath, but then he is a man who loves surprises.

My soft shade of hope flared into brighter tones of expectancy as he led me toward his pickup upon arrival, quietly suggesting we stop by the Rapid City courthouse to buy a marriage license, just in case. The white daisies he picked up at Safeway seemed to nod in brilliant affirmation of the plan afoot. As we arrived at the historic and seldom-used log chapel at Mystic, South Dakota, I knew a wedding was about to happen.

Pam Frink, the owner and caretaker, was just bustling out the door after sweeping up pine cones the squirrels had left inside. Stepping into the ancient log building was like walking into a painting Jon had created just for the occasion. Light streamed through antique windows, wooden pews waited empty, and a rustic cross beckoned us forward to the simple altar. Jon placed the flowers atop the wood stove, suspecting the service would be too short to worry about lighting a fire. Under my Texas-weight coat, I wore a long, navy blue, suede skirt with Texas-weight leather boots, the ones Jon always called city-slicker boots. I thought I might sing my vows to him, words of a song I had memorized on the plane the day before, hoping. But I was too cold, nervous, and emotional to sing solo in front of our two witnesses and the minister Jon had arranged to join us, so in a trembling voice I spoke the lyrics instead.

After our wedding at the Mystic Chapel. (Photo by Terry Hutchison.)

We are pilgrims on a journey.
We are travelers on the road.
We are here to help each other
Walk the mile and share the load.

I will weep when you are weeping.
When you laugh, I'll laugh with you.
I will share your joy and sorrow
'Til we've seen this journey through.

Will you let me be your servant?
Let me be as Christ to you.
Pray that I may have the grace
*To let you be my servant, too.**

His vows to me were spontaneous, unrehearsed, and perfectly natural, just like him. A man without pretense, he wears no jewelry, not even a watch, which meant he chose not to have a wedding band. Terry and Mary Lou Hutchison were our witnesses, and Terry videotaped the seven-minute service, a record of our vows. The words we spoke froze and lingered in the air as tangible evidence of our love. After the minister's benediction, the five of us gathered around the pickup outside for a tailgate marriage license signing on the edge of the snow-packed road.

*From "The Servant Songs," based on Isaiah.

-JON CRA
© 2012

OUR JOURNEY BEGINS

As we stood in front of the rustic chapel, now married, eyes shining, our breath billowing in the brittle morning air, I looked out toward the valley that would become our new home. The remoteness gave me a bit of a shiver, but the beauty was mesmerizing. I was aware that Pam Frink and her family lived near this intersection, where the road to Hill City passed the entrance into the Mystic Valley. Several families owned summer homes up the valley, and the path to it disappeared into the trees along the creek. I was pleased that my new husband had a blueprint in his head of the house he planned to build for us a couple of miles up that road, but I had no idea what life would be like there. I didn't know I would be living like a pioneer for the first several years of this journey. I didn't know I would live in a barn with concrete floors and no closets, learning as the early settlers did how to find water on our property. I didn't even know if we could get along together under the same roof, dirty socks and all, once real life began. I only knew I was deeply in love and that my James Avery gold wedding band spoke the promise to Jon that I intended to honor. "Whither thou goest, I will go." That dazzling morning, I meant those words with all my heart. There would be other less lustrous days to come, days when I would question my ability to keep that promise, as he led me far beyond the edge of my comfort zone.

I grew up a city girl. I lived in cities all my life until I married Jon. Midland, where I spent most of my youth, was an average-sized West Texas town that grew in fits and starts through the numerous

OPPOSITE *Down Castle Creek*, a watercolor by Jon Crane, depicting Castle Creek as it runs through the valley in the winter (2012).

I use the term "house of our dreams" lightly, admitting that I am not the dreamer. Still, those who know how to dream fascinate me. I am willing to stick around and watch a visionary work. My skill set is in adapting. He'd already finessed a level space large enough to hold a hot tub and a deck, so I watched Jon begin the improvements on his pristine hill, which plunged eighty feet down to a creek. I slid into the tub, enjoyed the view, and bought matching embroidered terry-cloth robes, just to be supportive. When he next added two more decks overlooking that sheer drop-off, but neglected to install railing, I gently insisted on railings before having any social gatherings, especially ones involving alcohol.

For the first summer after our wedding, we lived out of a pop-up camper, strategically placed next to the hot-tub deck, and we slept inside a tent on a king-sized, heated waterbed. My son, Michael, and Jon's son, Adam, shared another camper for the summer and helped on projects around the property. Come August, the boys went back to high school. Jon, Michael, and I returned to Midland, Texas, for the school term, and Adam went back to Montrose, Colorado, where he lived with his mom.

By the end of our second summer together, Jon and a group of his buddies had completed a barn-shaped structure for us to live in, "only until the main house is built in a year or two," or so he thought at the time. You might say that, since he had never built a house before, the barn was practice. We wanted it to be comfortable, but without frills, because it would be used as a garage and

OPPOSITE The road through the Mystic Valley.

Jon at “play” in his backhoe. (Photo by Gail Crane.)

Dakota woman I was becoming. Our first Thanksgiving at Mystic, I noticed the woodpile was low and grudgingly set out to take my turn on the splitter. After a morning of hoisting, splitting, and stacking, my mood had shifted from grudging and tense to grateful and calm, ready to participate in a Thanksgiving feast with a truly thankful spirit. I didn't even see it coming. Oddly enough, the thing I thanked God for the most that day was that hydraulic log splitter.

Jon and I worked together one January morning; I split and he stacked the wood neatly. Snow started falling as we worked, and Jon disappeared from time to time, returning just as I needed his help stacking. Three to four inches of snow accumulated as we stacked three to four feet of split wood, and again I found myself released of tension and contentedly surveying our woodpile. That evening, Jon showed me a video he had made through the day of me splitting wood in the falling snow—and singing the whole time. He had paired the video with the musical selection, "The Yellow Rose of Texas." He could hardly wait to share this glimpse into my new life with my Texas friends and family—who questioned my sanity in choosing such a lifestyle, in the back woods of South Dakota.

Our goal of building a real house within a couple of years did not happen. Business got in the way. We opened an art gallery in Hill City, seventeen miles away from home. For eight years, Jon continued painting, and I became consumed with selling his artwork in this new venue. We found no time to build a house, but we still took the time to travel. Together now, our vagabond spirits

Classic Jon Crane photo of an Amish farm in Ohio.

flourished, and we piled into our home on wheels, using any excuse we could find to hit the road.

Some of our travels centered on trade shows. We drove our motorhome, "Ed," along backroads to Chicago to exhibit Jon's work, stopping along the way to kayak in the Upper Mississippi Wildlife and Fish Refuge and pick wildflowers crowding the roadside to create a flower arrangement for our booth. Traveling the scenic secondary roads east to Valley Forge near Philadelphia, Pennsylvania, we ambled through the Amish countryside with Jon's camera clicking furiously, capturing nostalgic farms for future watercolors.We explored national forests and parks on the way to trade shows in Atlanta, New York, and Los Angeles, relying on Jon's well-trained sense of exploration to find beautiful and secluded campsites along the way. As a matter of fact, our love for America's national parks made getting older easier for me, knowing that eventually, at age 62, I could buy a lifetime Senior Parks Pass for ten bucks, allowing us free access to all our treasured National Parks.

Our other major incentive to travel was pure pleasure—the pleasure of cresting a hill and being lambasted with beauty along a quaint country road; the pleasure of capturing just the right light playing across an ordinary landscape, transforming it to extraordinary; the pleasure of regional foods and local brews; and the pleasure of swapping stories with strangers. We never tired of anticipating what we might find down those rugged dirt roads, the ones that were only broken lines on the map. Our collection of maps and *Gazetteers* kept growing, and so did my ability to read them. I tried to be helpful in the copilot's seat, but I am one of those directionally challenged travelers who has to hold the map upside down or sideways to fit my perception of where we are.

On one trip back to the east coast, before the era of cell phones and Google Maps, we were heading into and through a quaint Tennessee town with narrow streets and a busy downtown. The town was large enough to have its own little side map in the atlas. I studied the map carefully, planning the strategy we would need to get through and beyond the middle of town. All went well until we hit a crucial intersection where the road signs did not jive with my well-scripted plan. Nothing matched, and I could not tell Jon which way to turn. In a panic, I threw the map at him, announced that I quit my job as map reader, and sank into a my little girl pout deep in the seat, eyes closed and tears squeezing out the corners.

In disbelief, Jon turned the only way he could, and began doing what he does— following his nose. Unlike his copilot, he has

a well-developed sense of direction and instinctively knows how to factor in the sun, the way the wind is blowing, and how cities are put together. Before I knew it, we were out in the country, where he eventually stopped to calm me down. I apologized for being such a mess in a pinch. He said it all turned out fine in the end, adding with a grin, "By the way, quitting is not an option."

"Oh, yes it is," I responded, "at least for today. We'll see about tomorrow."

Try as we might, re-entry into real life at Mystic after a month or more away in the fall or winter was never easy. One particular year seemed especially difficult. Heading home from the southwest, I came down with a stomach bug. We got snowed in going through Colorado on our journey north. When we finally landed in the Black Hills, we were greeted with sub-zero temperatures and six to eight inches of new snow. Quite a shock for bodies that had been lulled into thinking it was already spring. The inevitable backlog of office, gallery, mail, and inventory issues pummeled us as we made our way through Hill City. Our arrival home to Mystic was a crash landing. The cistern had frozen because of a malfunctioning stock tank heater, so we had no water. The waterbed was chilly due to a worn-out heating element. The iron filter was unraveling because of extreme cold and insufficient draining. The woodpile was almost depleted, and the refrigerator was full of rotten food that we had forgotten to empty before departing. Encountering one disaster after another, we both became snarly, snarky, and totally frustrated.

Jon slept on the couch to keep the fire going that first night home, trying to warm up the frigid walls, furniture, and corners in the place. I slept on a mattress in the loft—the only other available bed that was not cold—and woke up not wanting to be there. We had too much repair work to do, too much that couldn't be done without water. Jon and I both were on a short fuse. I split logs for a while as Jon plowed a path through the snow. Then he drove to town for a stock-tank heater, a water-heater element, groceries, and drinking water, leaving me with a disaster to clean up.

His departure was for the best. He needed out from under the weight of my accusatory eyes that blamed him for the entire mess, and I needed relief from his frowning and gruff defenses. For the most part, I had become pretty adept at living this pioneer life, but that day I felt like cutting and running. It was more than I wanted to handle. How could I clean up this mess with no water? How could I begin bringing order into this chaos? How could I juggle the mounds of dirty clothes, the putrid refrigerator, the overflowing boxes of mail, the wine bottles that had popped their corks in the cold, and the jars of food that had frozen, broken, and oozed all over the dusty concrete floor?

All day I cleaned, using melted snow I warmed on the wood stove. Finally, in the late afternoon, I was drawn down to the deck overlooking the creek. My house was straight, but my heart was broken, and I began pouring out the bitter pieces before God. How long should I be expected to live like this, with so little order and

View of the cliff across the creek from our home.

so few amenities? Wood heat requiring back-breaking work. Cold concrete floors. Constant water problems. A husband's bad temper. Gently, God brought me to Himself. Gail, you chose to be Jon's helper and his friend. This is hard for him, too, and he needs you. Remember your wedding vows? You promised to help him walk the mile and share the load. Are you his supporter and friend only when you are lounging on a beach soaking up the sun? Or can you

also be his friend when he is down, disappointed, and depressed in the cold reaches of reality?

As I sat on the deck beneath the breathtaking beauty of our cliff, with the trees and the huge magnificent rocks standing guard over me, I was reminded of Psalm 121:

> *I lift my eyes to the hills, from where will my help come?*
> *My help comes from the Lord who made heaven and earth.*
> *He will not let your foot be moved;*
> *He who keeps you will not slumber.*
> *He who keeps Israel will neither slumber nor sleep.*
> *The Lord is your keeper!*

Soaking in the ancient words and nature's stillness, I felt my heart being stitched back together. I lifted my eyes up, away from the mess I was in and toward the majesty of God's creation, and I felt the stress of the day melt away. The beauty wooed me out of my misery and instructed my heart to know who would be my Provider, my Keeper, my Strength. The darkness fled, and I could not wait for my best friend to return home.

Pam Frink, the woman who had swept out the chapel the day of our wedding, lived a couple miles away with her husband, Russel, and son, Josiah, in circumstances not unlike my own. A few summer homes clung to the creek between their place and ours, but the Frinks were our closest year-round neighbors. They lived

Weathered Companions, a watercolor of historic buildings at Mystic by Jon Crane (2016).

in the house Russel was born in back in 1921, with only wood for heat, grandma's wood stove for cooking, a two-seater outhouse, and a beautiful historic setting along the creek. As we got to know them, they showed us photo albums and told stories that revealed the world that existed in this valley since the late 1800s. Hiking through the valley, we had stumbled across placer mines left gaping to the sky and railroad spikes scattered about, giving hints of the history. Conversations with Russ and Pam began to weave together a patchwork past of this quiet valley that had become our home.

Originally, this historic townsite north of Hill City was not even called Mystic. Before westward expansion brought railroads into the Black Hills, people referred to the area as Sitting Bull. Being a transplant to the Black Hills, I became curious about the origin of the name—and why it changed. But my research brought me no

clear answers. The legendary leader, Sitting Bull, was not born or buried here. And, although both the Cheyenne and Lakota tribes considered the Black Hills to be the spiritual center of the world, I found no evidence of a settlement that would have morphed into a mining town. So I invented small fictions to answer the question. Maybe a 1874 miner saw an outcropping that reminded him of a Native American profile. Or maybe, as I did, someone simply found the place inspiring, and harkened back to its Native roots.

My research did reveal some specific history that has stayed with me ever since. The first wave of mining fever brought on by George Custer's discovery of gold in 1874 lured thousands of eager miners into the hills. At the time, our little, remote valley suddenly burgeoned in population, as the tide pulled in railroad men, loggers, teachers, store clerks, and postmasters. When the first railroad line came through, the chief engineer on the survey crew, hailing from the east, suggested the name Mystic for the new station, and the name stuck.

Sitting in the quiet of the Frinks' kitchen, chatting over a cup of tea, I could hardly imagine the valley as it must have been then—with prospectors working up in the surrounding gulches, side by side, elbow to elbow, trying to dig their way into a pile of gold-rich gravel, what they called "pay dirt." As I looked out the window of their house, I saw little that remained physically to tell the mining story, other than the dilapidated assay office and a couple of run-down storage sheds. Larger mines with inscrutable names—

Lookout, Cuttysark, the Hack Tom, Mariposa Dickover, Fairview, Evans Dredge, and Inca—all faded into the fabric of a rugged, yet romantic, past. Even the grandest mining story in the valley, the Electro-Chemical Reduction Plant, disappeared without a trace. The plant was a massive and imposing structure designed to extract gold by electro-cyanide or electro-chlorination processes. Unfortunately, after four years of experimentation, the process that worked well in a laboratory was abandoned. The million-dollar mill was torn down because it did not function on a large commercial scale.

The one thing that did remain after the Electro-Chemical Reduction Plant was demolished was the old gold mill foundation. There it sat, waiting to be transformed. Turns out, a man named George Frink was ready for a new endeavor, and Mystic was ready for a new venture.

In 1901, at the age of ten, George rode the train alone from Chicago with a note pinned on his shirt that said "Mystic." The conductors made sure he arrived safely, and William Frink, his father, was at the train station to meet him. William had been an architect in North Chicago. He had a college education and was also trained as a baker, in case he was ever to "get on his uppers," an expression his grandson Russel explained as walking around in worn-out shoes with no soles, only uppers. In the Panic of 1893, that must have been what happened. After some years as a successful architect, but with financial hard times at his door, he quit the faltering building-trades industry and followed the siren

OPPOSITE Historic building still remaining at Mystic.

George Frink Sawmill at Mystic, 1920. (Photo from the Russel Frink Collection.)

song of the Black Hills. He left his family for a while around 1897, traveling alone out to Mystic, where he invested in the emerging commerce of the area. He bought a grocery store, started baking, and bought stock in the experimental gold mill, revealing a deep belief in the potential of the area. In 1901, he sent for his young son, George, and the rest of the family eventually followed. They all lived in the back of the grocery store. By 1918, George was twenty-seven years old, and someone had built a sawmill on that old gold mill foundation. The next year, George was able to buy the sawmill and it became his livelihood for thirty-six years. This new industry changed the landscape at Mystic.

George's son, Russel, was born in the family's new home, the former superintendent's house at Mystic. After leaving home and living for many years elsewhere, Russel returned again to the same house, where he lived with his wife, Pam, and their son, Josiah. When I was new to the area, that house, and the hot tea within it, became landmarks for me as I learned my way around. As I turned off the Mystic road and up toward our valley, the house stood right there with its familiarity and warmth, assuring me that I was almost home. In 1995, the house burned down one Wednesday evening while the Frinks were at church. Even though I was comfortable finding my way without it by then, Jon and I, along with all our neighbors, mourned with the Frinks over the loss of not only a home, but a treasure chest of historic nuggets.

images of mystic

COUNTRY LIVING

chapter two

One of my biggest adjustments to the edges of country living was driving on country roads. Jon chose to live at Mystic for many reasons, one of which was the seclusion, which meant living at the end of a gravel or dirt road. In our case, that gravel road was often and decidedly covered with ice or snow. Seclusion, gravel, ice, and snow all added up to breath-holding and white-knuckle driving for this Texan.

Truth be told, I have occasionally found some magic in the challenge of South Dakota's bad-weather driving, like the evening Jon and I were in Hill City, ready to drive the road home. As we left town, snow began to gently fall, but within minutes, the gentle snow turned into a full-blown blizzard. Jon did not even blink, but for me, panic set in. Big, windy snow always assails me with images of pioneers dying a few feet from their house because of disorientation and freezing conditions. Thankfully, Jon knows how to drive like a South Dakotan. He also understands me like he understands road maps, and that evening he read my anxiety. Turning off the paved Deerfield Road onto the gravel toward Mystic, he cheerily said, "A couple of more miles will get us to that house on the left, and if we need to, we can stop there." I nodded in increasing panic, and he opened his door to keep his eye on the edge of the road.

I instructed myself to breathe. As we drove past the house on the left, Jon continued his soothing chatter, as one might encourage a two-year-old just learning to swim. "We're doing just fine. Let's head on toward the Kaubisch Ranch. That's not far, and I'm sure

Mallet engine #4108 at the Mystic Station, 1941. (Photo from the Russel Frink Collection.)

they wouldn't mind if we needed to stop there." He opened his window and flicked the windshield wipers to clear the mounting snow. We crept on.

I knew that the distance from the Kaubisch Ranch to the next point of civilization was a long way. As we rounded the curve up and beyond the Kaubisch turnoff, I squinted through the windshield and peered at Jon, wondering if the storm might be letting up. "Yep, I'm pretty sure that snow is easing up. Let's get to that trailhead up the road a way and reassess," he quipped. He fiddled with the lights, trying to decide whether high or low beams worked better in a blizzard. I could not see through that white curtain either way.

But he was right. As we proceeded through the blizzard, opening the doors to check the edges, flicking the wipers, and finally settling on dim beams, we noticed a light beginning to peer through from above. Snow and wind diminished, then stopped altogether, and as we inched around the corner toward Castleton, a benevolent full moon pierced the night, flooding the meadow with a soft radiance. Jon turned off the wipers, shut off the headlights, and we laughed our way home to Mystic by moonlight.

I try to imagine what it was like to live at Mystic before the invention of automobiles or phones, and my brain gets tangled up thinking about it. That would be seclusion beyond my power to visualize. I have heard a few stories from friends who grew up there, like Jay Hendrickson, who moved to the area in 1929. In March, his family moved into a log house with no plumbing or electricity and with snow hanging from the trees. By the time they moved to this isolated edge of civilization, the train had come to town and dispelled part of the sense of isolation that had earlier prevailed. The Chicago, Burlington and Quincy Railroad, also known as CB&Q, reached Mystic on its way from Edgemont to Deadwood in 1890. Known also as the High Line, the Burlington, or later the Burlington Northern, the CB&Q, opened the picturesque Mystic valley to the wide world beyond. Commodities such as lumber, gold and silver ore, or coal from Wyoming could reach their destinations efficiently and more economically than ever before.

In 1906, an additional link in this transportation grid was added, enhancing commerce and tourism to the east. The Rapid City, Black Hills & Western Railroad, also known as the Missouri River & Northwestern, finally made its way to Mystic from Rapid City on the eastern edge of the Black Hills. I am not sure what it means when a railroad is known by ten different nicknames, but such was the case for this particular road. Some locals called the RCBH&W "Rattle, Clatter, Bump Hard, and Wiggle" or "Rough Crooked Big Hills and Wrecks." It was often referred to by the shorter name of The Dakota and Wyoming, made shorter as The D&W, and made more descriptive as the "Dusty & Windy." One common name was The Crouch Line, paying homage to one of the early investors, and the most affectionate name was The Dinky. The Dinky ran thirty miles from Rapid City on the eastern edge of the Black Hills to Mystic, for the purpose of transporting coal, timber, ore, and passengers. The route was short, circuitous, and frequently in need of repair, because it crossed water 110 times on bridges that were subject to flooding. When the train reached Mystic, it was at the end of the line and had to turn around to head back to Rapid City. For a short distance as it came into Mystic, it shared the track of the CB&Q, making for an interesting choreography of communicating and coordinating time, disconnecting cars, turning around, reconnecting cars, offloading commodities or passengers, loading up, and heading out again.

Jay Hendrickson's family arrived from Huron on this train. His father, Jack, worked cutting logs at George Frink's sawmill and did carpentry work as the settlement developed. Even though most people had very little materially, they managed to have fun, all the same. Per young Jay, child-sized adventures included fishing, of course, as well as running the ridges above town, rolling rocks over the edges, and chasing cows. The forest had been leased for cattle grazing by that time, which involved cowboys on horseback coming in to work the herd. Watching the action was a sheer wonder for a child, like going to a rodeo. Jay confessed with a twinkle in his eye that Granddad Barker had a powder house where he stored dynamite. There were rumors of kids snitching dynamite to use in blasting old tree roots and big rocks that just needed blasting.

Beginning at a tender age, everyone pitched in to make life work, day to day. Jay's parents depended on him to hoe the weeds in the potato patch and to chop wood for winter warmth. He could earn money by cutting pitch posts, shoveling sawdust at the sawmill, and removing rocks from the road. He remembers carrying baggage for passengers who came in on the train and also delivering goods that arrived by train to local residents. When the moms ordered school clothes—by sending a Sears catalogue order to Denver by train on Monday—the order would come in on Wednesday's train, and Jay would deliver it. Even doing a little panning for gold could earn enough money for a candy splurge at the Mystic store now and then.

When Jay began school after moving to Mystic, he, Russ Frink, and others from around the area joined the ranks of country kids everywhere who had to walk a mile or two each way to school. The closest school at that time was the Gilbert school at Castleton, about a mile and a half south of Mystic. The teacher taught eight grades in one room, with children funneling in from Pony Gulch, Hoodoo Gulch, Wheeler Gulch, Bluebird Gulch, Bittersweet Gulch, Brown Jug, and Wildcat Gulch, to name a few. Eventually, a school

Historic photo of the Mystic School. (Photo from the Russel Frink Collection.)

was opened at Mystic, where Jay attended classes through his ninth-grade year.

Those were the years of the Great Depression. Work was scarce and money was hard to come by, but during that time of scarcity, Jay does not remember ever feeling poor. People were self-sufficient, surviving on crops they grew or on local game and fish. Squatters came to claim and live on parcels of land without any formal agreements, especially during the '30s, when they were forced off the drought-stricken prairies of South Dakota. Every gulch burgeoned with small cabins where people lived almost for free, hauling water from local springs, picking berries, fishing the streams, and sometimes trying their hand at panning for gold. Isolated living conditions were primitive, as were the roads, but folks linked arms, depended on themselves, knew how to lend a hand, and made do.

Jay's family remained in Mystic until 1940. During the eleven years of their residency, Jack and the boys were not the only ones working outside the Hendrickson home. Jay's mom, Mary, also found ways to help put bread on the table. She and Irene Frink, Russ's aunt, ran a restaurant for passengers coming in on the train. They served food only at noon, which, no doubt included wild game from the forest and potatoes from Mary's own garden. In addition, she became the local midwife, bringing at least a dozen babies into their new world at Mystic. On each of those occasions, she might have been away from home for several days.

On September 5, 1932, Mrs. Hendrickson assisted Mrs. Millicent Brown in the delivery of her eleventh and last baby, Jim Brown. Jim's sister, Margaret, remembers well the day he was born. The one-room school had a new teacher that year, and ten-year-old Margaret had volunteered to help her clean the school in preparation for their first day of class. As she came home from a long day of scrubbing, polishing, and sprucing up, she discovered she had a new baby brother, and he was sleeping in her doll bed.

Jim and Margaret's father, Walter, worked for the railroad, living in Mystic during summer months and Edgemont in the winter, nearly seventy miles away on the southern edge of the Black Hills. According to Russel Frink, "Millie Brown was the chief instigator of God's work in Mystic." Up until 1930, churchgoers had been meeting in the homes of the faithful for worship. In 1930, a woman from Philadelphia named Miss McCahan learned, through missionary work done by the Presbytery of South Dakota, of the need for funds for a chapel at Mystic. She donated those

=Post=Office.

funds. The Frink sawmill and men of the community provided lumber and labor, and a horse-drawn plow leveled the ground. The McCahan Memorial Chapel became a reality and was dedicated as a non-denominational chapel on Thanksgiving Day of 1931. Millie Brown was very involved in the programs of the new church, and young Jim Brown became one of only a few youngsters listed on the cradle roll, as the babies in the congregation were called.

As a young boy, Jim would attend church with his family, where he learned his Sunday School verses, went to vacation bible school, and participated in special events such as the Christmas program. One especially memorable Christmas event included the holiday tradition of lighting the church by decorating the Christmas tree with lit candles. Victor Redding, a cousin of Russel Frink, picked one of the candles off the tree, and in the process caught his clothes on fire. Luckily, his quick-thinking aunt pulled the blazing boy out the door and rolled him in the snow to drench the flames.

By the time Jon and I were married in the Mystic Chapel, services were no longer being held there, and it was only used for an occasional special event or wedding like ours.

We do know a couple that was among the first to be married there. The same Jim Brown who was on the cradle roll at Mystic's new church in 1932 married his sweetheart, Carolyn, at a summer wedding in 1956. The chapel was filled with local wildflowers, and the altar was beautifully decorated with candles. As romantic as the setting was, the most memorable part of the service came when a

OPPOSITE Historic photo of the Mystic Post Office. (Photo from the Russel Frink Collection.)

packrat made his entrance, no doubt curious about what was going on in his living room. Luckily, the moment his head peeked out, the soloist hit a high note that sent the little critter scurrying for cover back down the hole. Years later, the Brown's daughter upheld the family tradition and was also married in the tiny Mystic Chapel. The packrat clan upheld its end of the tradition as well by sending in one of the family to attend. This time the packrat was scared away by the pounding of grandpa's cane.

To get from the chapel at the historic Mystic town site to our home in the Mystic valley a couple of miles away, we initially drove on the old railroad bed. The Crouch Line was abandoned in 1942, and the Burlington Northern shut down in 1983, due to declining cargo and increased maintenance. The abandoned railroad bed made a nice, easy grade for vehicles to access the private properties that began developing in the valley. However, one of the biggest problems would occur during mud season, as winter released its icy hold and the ground began to thaw. Driving in mud proved to be as treacherous as driving on ice.

During one of my first springs in Mystic, I decided I could tackle a drive north to the faded mining settlement of Rochford, known best for the Moonshine Gulch Saloon, to do a pressing errand. The drive out to Mystic was slippery and unpredictable, as expected. The road north to Rochford was graveled, which provides traction against the mud of the season. After attending to my business and before leaving Rochford, I called Jon to tell him I

OPPOSITE McCahan Memorial Chapel at Mystic.

An icy road near Rochford, close to our home at Mystic.

was on my way home and to alert him to come looking for me stuck in the mud if he did not see me in half an hour. Before reaching the real mud pit between Mystic and home, something splattered all over my windshield. I jerked to a stop, stunned, and saw a snowball dripping slowly down the glass. From off the hill and out of the trees trotted my husband, all grins, very pleased to have hit his target and caught my attention so effectively. "Could you use a little help driving through that mud?" he innocently inquired. I couldn't decide whether to be upset or relieved, but I chose relieved, and gratefully let him slide behind the wheel.

In 1997, Jon was commissioned to paint a Christmas tree—not just any tree, but a special spruce selected to go from the Black Hill National Forest to Washington, D.C. The People's Tree would adorn the Capitol lawn for the holiday season. Jon's painting was to be used as a fundraiser to help pay for the transportation costs of getting the tree across the country. One of our perks was an invitation to attend the tree lighting ceremony in Washington, to be held in November.

On an icy morning a few days before our flight to Washington, I was driving out of the valley toward our gallery in Hill City. As I neared one of the blind curves on the railroad bed we used as our road, I suddenly saw a pickup coming at me very fast. Before I could react, we hit head-on, knocking me thirty feet back. The most lasting injury—more enduring than my whiplash and a totaled Jeep—was finding out that the men in the pickup were coming into the valley to survey for the newly proposed Rails to Trails project, an effort that we initially did not support. Jon purchased property in the valley specifically because it was secluded and private. In our thinking, a recreational trail would obliterate our privacy and end our peace and quiet.

I wore a neck brace for several weeks, including during the trip to Washington for the tree-lighting ceremony. Even after my neck healed, I still felt bruised by the irony of who hit me. Our spirits continued to resist the whole idea of a trail intruding upon our protected little paradise, even as plans were approved and put into motion.

Months later, I was again driving out of the valley, when I was hit once more, but this time with words. "The earth is the Lord's, and the fullness thereof, the world and all that dwell therein." Again, I was stopped dead in my tracks. Why had the words of

-JON CRANE-
©1997

this familiar Psalm suddenly popped into my head? "Okay," I said, looking up. "I'm listening."

Child, do you honestly believe you own this road, or the property where you live? You actually do not own any part of this valley. You have some land to use for a while, but really, it all belongs to Me. You do not have a right to keep others from enjoying what I have made. The beauty I have created here is for your refuge and renewal, but it is for the renewal of others as well. Open up your tight fist and let it go.

Since that day, we quit fighting the Mickelson Trail. As a matter of fact, Jon supported it by painting a couple of trail scenes and donating some of the proceeds from print sales for trail maintenance. In 2016, on Jon's fortieth anniversary as an artist, the South Dakota Parks Department dedicated the tunnel closest to our home to Jon for his support of the trail and his dedication to his art. And we found a bit of irony in this situation, too, but for the good. What we assumed would bring a negative influence into our lives ended up being a major plus. The sounds we hear on the nearby trail include laughter, happy chatter, and the spin of bicycle wheels as they cruise through a section of God's stunning handiwork.

Even so, God was not finished with our lessons. For forest dwellers—both visitors and permanent residents—fire is an ever-present threat. At the time of the devastating southern Black Hills Jasper Fire in August of 2000, my job became transportation of artwork and the cat. The fire actually blazed twenty miles south

OPPOSITE *America's Holiday Tree*, a watercolor by Jon Crane, shows the People's Tree that was sent to Washington D.C. from the Black Hills (1997).

of our Mystic place, but only ten miles from the Hill City Gallery, and we did not know from day to day which direction the wind was going to blow. We had to be on alert at all times to evacuate in either location. I loaded up my Jeep with Jon's original artwork from the gallery and his family heritage art collection from the house, carrying the load back and forth as I came and went to work each day. When I left the gallery in the evenings, Callie, the gallery cat, came with me to the house, and back we both went to the gallery every morning. That fire became the largest wildfire in the history of the Black Hills, devastating more than 83,000 acres. Thankfully, firefighters contained it within a few days, and I was finally able to unload my cargo and the cat, but I was never able to shake that uneasy feeling of impending disaster from fire.

We see evidence of lightning strikes in the charred remains of pine trees in numerous places on our property. One summer day in 2017, Jon gave me a call in my Hill City office to say I might want to get home in a hurry to help him pack up what we should save in case we had to evacuate. A lightning strike up on a ridge about a mile away from our house had become a conflagration, and the fire department had been summoned.

I sped toward home, eyes trained on the mountaintop, as I made my way through the Mystic Valley. And there it was, smoke billowing and flames flaring, threatening several homes that were closer than our own. When I drove into the driveway, Jon said he had led the firefighters to the closest place for them to park, to begin

OPPOSITE The Mickelson Trail winding its way through the Mystic Valley.

-JON CRANE-
© 1998

their hike toward the flames. We drove back over to keep an eye on their progress from a closer vantage point.

That year was also the tenth year of the massive pine-bark beetle infestation, an epidemic that affected the entire Black Hills. We watched with great sadness as giant swaths of lush green gave way to the brown ravages of a tiny beetle made powerful against Ponderosa Pines weakened by drought. We came to understand that a healthy forest needs fire or regular thinning to keep from becoming overpopulated, spindly, and unhealthy. The bark beetle is one way Mother Nature thins out an overgrown forest, creating what some would call a slow burn.

Watching the ridge fire burn on that summer day, I struggled to be positive about the drama being played out before me. I found it easy to be grateful for the yellow-clad troops who trudged up the hill, weighted down with gear, putting our safety before their own. Of course the next day, knowing the fire was out and we did not have to flee before the flames, relief and gratitude flooded over us. Academically, I know the fire was pruning and mending the forest, just like the slow burn of the bark beetle. Emotionally then, I too am probably being pruned as I learn to trust the lightning, the fire, and the perfectly balanced creative forces of our earth home.

OPPOSITE *In Good Company*, a watercolor by Jon Crane, commemorating the George S. Mickelson Trail (1998).

returned from town with grocery supplies, including Fudgesicles for the kids, and they had to be eaten before they melted.

While Bill ran the grocery store, George operated the sawmill known as the Mystic Tie and Logging Company. George also built up another business that helped to nurture tourism in the area. He owned an assortment of vacation cabins designed to house the increasing number of travelers coming to Mystic by train. He called the cabins Green Tree Camp. Built between 1929 and 1930, the six cabins ranged in price from 50 cents to $1 per night per guest. Beverly Manor, The House in the Pines, and The Cedar Chest could accommodate four or more guests at a weekly rate of $10. All cabins, except the tiny Doll House, which was for sleeping only, were equipped with dishes and cooking utensils. However, bedding for any of the cabins would cost an extra 25 cents per bed. The promotional brochure extolled the rustic beauty and woodland seclusion, the proximity to fishing streams, a grocery store, and a post office, as well as a central location convenient by motor car to all points of interest in the Hills.

In an article published by the Northwestern Bell News on August 6, 1980, George Frink recalled that around 1910 the first toll line for telephone service was built as an exchange between Hill City and Deadwood. The line provided local exchange services for area telephone customers until the late 1970s. In typical George Frink fashion, he took on the community responsibility of running the toll center from his home, which also was the headquarters for

OPPOSITE An image capturing the rustic beauty of Mystic.

Calvin and Grace Coolidge at Mystic, being transported by George Frink in his lumber wagon. (Photo from the Russel Frink Collection.)

his lumber business. He remembered it this way:

"I got a monthly commission of $1.50 from Bell for taking care of calls, timing conversations and keeping other records. We had a lot more people living and working here back then. Whenever there was an incoming call, I'd have to run out and fetch the person while the other party waited on the line. I was authorized to charge my own messenger fee but, what the heck, I never did."

In the same article, George reminisced about an event at Mystic that brought national attention to the little mountain settlement. Calvin and Grace Coolidge came to town to visit Nebraska's Governor, Samuel McKelvie, at his summer home on Slate Creek near Mystic.

"One day he (Coolidge) visited Mystic and I was in charge of transportation for him and his wife. It was a big old lumber wagon pulled by two horses. We fished, panned for gold, and did some hiking into the Hills. That Coolidge, he was tougher than hell. He was one president who didn't chew his cabbage twice."

(To spare you, dear reader, from Googling that term, I'll share my research with you. "Didn't chew his cabbage twice" meant "refused to repeat himself." Whatever he said, you'd better catch it the first time around. I might also add the intriguing rumor among family and friends that some dandelion wine had been imbibed along the creek that day, and Grace appeared not to have been too happy about it.)

President and Mrs. Coolidge spent most of the summer of 1927 in the Black Hills, setting up a summer White House in Custer State Park. On July 23, the following article appeared in the *Belvidere* (Illinois) *Daily Republican*, written by George E. Durno:

Mystic, S. D., July 23—Calvin Coolidge, undisputed movie star of the Black Hills went on "location" today.

Accompanied by his personal movie men and a large corps of correspondents, the president came 35 miles up Rapid Canyon this morning to this little jumping off place on French Creek, here to record once and for all the picture for which there have been two seasons of rehearsal—the chief executive of the United States, hip boots, rod and reel, at the business of casting for, striking and pulling in a trout from the mountain stream.

It was a little over a year ago that Mr. Coolidge, fresh from Washington where he had referred to fishing as child's play, arrived at Paul Smith's, N.Y., for his annual vacation, was persuaded to try his luck with hook and line, and became a confirmed disciple of Izaak Walton. The movie men and photographers pursued him all of (the) 1926 season beseeching him for a picture but without avail and since his arrival in the Black Hills this year they have cast longing eyes in the direction of Squaw Creek—now officially dubbed "Grace Coolidge" Creek—with no more success.

But this morning the word went out at Mystic the long-awaited-for picture would be available and the news reel boys were on hand with hundreds of feet of film in their magazines.

Newspapers from far and wide carried stories about Coolidge's visit to Mystic, sending out reports to their reading public about the wild grandeur of the Black Hills. By the end of the next day, Americans were convinced that Mystic was a desirable, though untamed, recreational destination where fish were abundant and gold lay waiting to be discovered. The reports also made clear that, although the fish were not biting for the president that day, due to high muddy waters of recent rains, their man Coolidge knew how to fly-fish.

According to family lore, George and Bill Frink were not the best of friends, but they did manage to work together occasionally. One common enterprise was making moonshine. The story goes that they made the moonshine for their own amusement, but Bill Frink's wife did not find it to be all that amusing. For example, there must have been some heavy sampling going on the day Bill Frink went blind. His vision was impaired for three days, at which point Irene poured the brew out into her mop bucket. One has to wonder whether that put a halt to the enterprise all together, and whether the moonshine took the shine off her floor.

Mystic was a small but busy commercial hub until the middle of the century, when commerce eventually switched gears, slowed down, and ground to a halt. In 1942, the Crouch Line into Rapid City was abandoned. By 1955, George Frink's sawmill was shut down after nearly forty years in operation. Bill Frink closed his grocery store in 1970 and the building was moved to Hill City, where it served several other purposes, including a small market, a survey call center and a storage room. Currently, the building resides next to the Chute Rooster Restaurant and dreams of fancy groceries and little kids licking Fudgesicles on the porch. The last passenger train on the Burlington Railroad ran in 1947, and the last freight train came through in 1983. Mystic napped for a few quiet years, and when she awoke, she was no longer who she used to be. The earth beneath her no longer shook with passing trains. Her ear was not razored with train whistles. Sawdust did not cling to her hair, and saws' buzzing did not set her teeth on edge.

To the miners of the late nineteenth century, Mystic made promises of wealth that she could not keep, and most miners vanished, disillusioned. Pioneers and entrepreneurs from the first half of the twentieth century approached her looking for food,

Wildlife lends a deep layer of beauty for those who come seeking.

survival, and commerce, but the dreams she nurtured were fleeting and faded like photos left in the sun. Then came those seeking only her beauty, and they have stayed for generations. Her beauty is reliable and solid, crafted as a never-ending gift for those who seek her. Her spell remains.

Jon was among those who came to Mystic seeking that beauty and inspiration. He called her his Mystic Mistress, and she dazzled him from their first encounter. I arrived more like the plains pioneers who straggled in to escape drought and to find newness of life. Emotionally, my life was parched and I was not sure what I needed to survive. Jon Crane held out his hand to me and drew me into his dreams along the edge of nature's beauty, where my renewal began.

Jon called me on the phone from home one summer day while I was working in our Hill City Gallery, asking a rather odd question. "How well do you like country living?" he queried. I assured him that I would not trade my country home for anything on earth.

By that time, our dream house had finally been completed and we had settled into it with deep sighs of belonging and comfort. We would always have little projects to do, because Jon is a dreamer, a visionary whose creative bent pushes him relentlessly toward invention. That pile of bricks left over after installing the kitchen, mudroom, and front entry floors had to be used, so plans swirled in his mind about barbecues, smokers, basement walls, and bread ovens. Every spring, a new crop of garden improvements flourished in his fertile imagination, until the humble sixteen-foot-square patch of soil grew into a complex with a greenhouse, garden shed, fence, raised beds, and expanded perimeters. He dreamed about building a root cellar for all the fresh produce, and he constantly rearranged the driveways around the property with his backhoe to accommodate the improvements.

Each time Jon completed an addition to the design, I tumbled more deeply into a state of wonder. I had learned to trust his instincts about living well out in the wilds, and so his question about how I liked the country sparked my curiosity. "Why do you ask?" I ventured.

"Well, because part of the country has come inside today," he said obliquely.

The home of our dreams, with wildflowers rather than grass to tend.

"Are you telling me we have another packrat infestation?" I blurted, assailed with vivid memories of our ongoing rodent battles.

"No, actually, today we have a bunny in the basement, and I can't figure out how to get him out without scaring the little guy."

When I arrived home, Jon was in the process of trying to gently herd our new resident back out the door. As he nudged the unexpected guest toward the basement door at the end of the hall, it darted into the utility room instead, where there were plenty of hiding places and much to explore. Jon blocked off the hallway and tied a rope to the open utility room door. He then brought the rope over the blockade into the center room. He made our guest comfortable by providing lettuce, carrots, and water on the floor in the hall. When the bunny finally ventured out into the hall to munch lettuce for breakfast the next morning, Jon was waiting. He gently pulled the utility room door closed, called me down to say goodbye, and then went around the outside of the house to open the hall doorway. We both watched from a distance as our furry companion sniffed the fresh air and followed his nose out the open door.

Sometimes our visitors are not as benign as a bunny. One December, wild turkeys found their way onto our back deck. Turkeys are among the few feathered friends that are not welcome at our bird feeders. They have small featherless heads like buzzards, leave a large gooey mess like geese, and because of their size, chase off all the other birds feeding, like hawks do. We discovered they are quite tenacious once they find a free breakfast and do not scare away easily. Even shooting a gun close to their feet would not deter them for long.

One dawn, after a couple of weeks of trying to discourage the raids, Jon caught a flock of turkeys at the bird feeders and, at his approach, they fled. As usual, he prepared to blast away near their feet to underscore his displeasure, but the birds suddenly exploded into action, flying, squawking, trembling, and hiding as high or as far as their panic would take them. Keeping his eyes trained on the scene, he finally saw the cause of the chaos. A mountain lion stealthily slunk through the early morning space where the turkeys had been. Dashing into the house, Jon exchanged the gun for a camera, woke me up with his urgent whispers to follow him, and ran back into the kitchen to shoot three low-light and fuzzy photos through the kitchen window. My wide eyes caught Jon's as we both silently acknowledged the same thought. If this intruder does not deter the turkeys, nothing will.

Our resident rabbit captured Jon's heart and became the subject of his painting entitled *Garden Companion* (2014).

Unfortunately, we were wrong. The lion made his exit without a kill, and soon after, the turkeys came marching back down the hill. Several more days of loud gun noises finally convinced the birds they were not welcome on our deck, and they disappeared. Maybe the mountain lion eventually got to them. I must admit he definitely got to me, leaving my psyche unsettled and nervous. We have always known of their presence in our area and love knowing they are here, but we take care to keep walks in the darkness to a minimum, knowing they are typically nocturnal. We have had numerous sightings of them and their tracks on our property or in close proximity, but seeing one so close to our kitchen was unnerving.

Educating myself about the local wildlife became a survival technique for living on this edge of wildness. Regarding mountain lions, I read that the wrong thing to do when encountering one would be to run, appearing to be prey. The right thing to do would be to "make big" and roar loudly in place while staring the lion down. In other words, do the opposite of what your instincts tell you to do. I hope I never have to test this theory.

On snowy winter hikes, we often see tracks of deer, rabbits, and the occasional coyote. Squirrels, chipmunks, and raccoons are constant sources of entertainment in the warmer months. At times, we hear rocks clattering on the cliff across the creek, sending a signal to us to grab our binoculars and scan the cliff for bighorn sheep or mountain goats. Once we peered out the bedroom window, still groggy from our night's sleep, and thought we were hallucinating. The entire cliff was in motion. Rubbing our eyes and looking closer, we realized the movement was a huge herd of big horn sheep, ambling in unison across the jagged rock face. Knowing we were witnessing a rare event in our world, we watched them for a long time as they made their way up over the crest of the mountain.

My growing fascination with the creatures of the wild around Mystic kept me from feeling oppressed by our remote location. The sight of the belted kingfisher swooping toward the creek for fish, the bleating of the lambs demanding their supper, the tickle of a chipmunk's fur as he furtively grabbed sunflower seeds from my hand, the lyrical notes of the canyon wren as she bid us good evening—all of these diverted my attention from the void of human activity that otherwise might have overwhelmed me.

TOP A female bighorn sheep eyes us from her cliff perch.
BOTTOM A mountain goat looks quizzically across the creek to our deck.

In reality, though, we also have had a loose net of human neighbors who occupy the summer homes near us. Although I cannot see them from our place, I know they are just over the hill, and especially in the summer months, we share life in this tiny community. We know we can count on someone nearby for that needed cup of sugar or for that the extra muscle to lift a fallen tree off the road.

The year Jon was building our fireplace in the living room, I asked him repeatedly what he planned to use for the mantel, which would have to be nine feet wide. Repeatedly, he shrugged his shoulders. One day, when the base was finally ready for the mantel, two buddies, Rich and Paco, drove up the driveway with a gigantic piece of slate protruding from the bed of the pickup they were driving. As they had driven into our valley, Rich spotted this extraordinary rock jutting out of the mountainside, and it caught his imagination. Would it possibly work as a mantel? With the help of gravity, he and Paco coaxed the giant rock off the mountain and into the pickup bound for our home. What a gift from Mother Nature and our friends. The slab measured exactly nine feet wide, was perfectly flat, and needed only to be power washed to gain mantel status. Then we called for help from our community. Every man in the valley helped hoist it into place.

Mother Nature felt less friendly in October of 2013, when the Atlas Storm hit western South Dakota. The storm was in the forecast, and as we watched it develop, we canceled plans that would

Gail's son, Michael, practices total stillness to attract hungry chipmunks to sunflower seeds.

have kept us in Rapid City for the weekend and stayed at home. In our valley in the central Black Hills, we ended up with three feet of new snow, trees felled by high winds that blocked our access in and out of the valley, power lines snapped and dangling, and twenty people trapped in their summer cabins with little preparation for an extended stay. The snow was so high and heavy that we could not get to our closest neighbors to offer assistance.

Our house was fine in such conditions, because Jon designed it with a fireplace and wood stoves, as well as a cistern that could gravity-feed into the utility room in the basement. We were able to get plenty of water by the bucket, and the woodshed was well stocked. Being without power for a couple of days was a romantic adventure, and we used candlelight for dining and our camping lights to cook, clean up, and read. Amazingly, we did not lose our phone service, and we were able to keep the computers charged in our solar-powered camper.

After five days, the adventure lost its luster. Luckily, the fifth day was our day of liberation, when someone came into our valley with a huge six-wheel-drive road grader to clear our road of deep snow and downed trees so we could begin to move about. People fled from the valley like birds freed from a cage. Finally, on day twelve, the power company reached us at the end of the line, and our electricity was restored.

In the middle of all that inconvenience, I was feeling oddly downcast, edgy. I tried to buck up. As I trudged through the snow on the road near our house, I kept spotting young spruce trees bent over, their tops still weighted down with heavy, wet snow. As I passed, I would lift them up out of the snow, brush them off, and encourage them to stand straight again, seeking the sun. I thought about them later that morning as I meditated on a passage from

scripture, which said, "So if you're serious about living this new resurrection life with Christ, act like it....Don't shuffle along, eyes to the ground, absorbed with the things right in front of you. Look up, and be alert to what is going on around Christ—that's where the action is. See things from His perspective" (Colossians 3: 1-2 in *The Message*). I sensed my Heavenly Father's loving care as he lifted me up out of my snowy doldrums, brushed off the heavy weight of worry, and realigned my gaze upward toward Him.

OPPOSITE The mantel for our fireplace was well worth waiting for.

OPPOSITE A young spruce tree laden with snow seeks the sun.

images of baja

FIRST IMPRESSIONS

chapter four

Our 1991 Ford pickup was topped with a pop-up camper bulging with everything we might possibly need in Mexico. This was our first road trip to Baja, so in addition to necessities—maps, charts, books, and clothes—we stuffed in a GPS, weather radios, snorkeling gear, water-proof bags, a beach umbrella, Jon's portable easel, a Spanish dictionary, a guest tent, a rock hammer, and two bright red kayaks precariously perched on top. The Immigration Office in Tecate was not yet open as we crossed the border, so we were diverted south to Ensenada to buy our tourist cards. With some trepidation on my part, we rolled slowly through the sleepy town, headed south with the first light of the new day.

We had been married for three years when we made this initial leap into Baja. In the years I had known Jon, I was getting used to traveling back roads, living miles from the closest grocery store, reading road maps, and cutting wide swaths around civilization in favor of the simpler life on the edge of it. In preparation for this trip, our Mystic home became littered with guide books and maps that opened my eyes to the finer points of negotiating the 1,000-mile peninsula tailing off from the southern border of California. I must admit I did not know where Baja was before we launched our first trip down. I was not even sure whether it was in the United States or Mexico. Jon was the only person I knew who had ever been there, but even he had not driven down the peninsula. He had only flown down to the tip to go deep-sea fishing years ago with some of his buddies. Ever cautious, I could not help but wonder whether a trip into Baja would be safe.

After crossing into Mexico through the small town of Tecate, we traveled west on Highway 3 toward the bustling city of Ensenada. When we caught our first view of the Pacific Ocean, Jon was torn between gazing at the dazzling expanse of water and negotiating the busy traffic as we turned south along Highway 1. I was feeling nervous about subjecting anyone to my Spanish, because it had been twenty years since I had spoken a word of it, but in the Immigration Office, I gave it a try. The moment this blue-eyed blonde attempted Spanish, the officer's demeanor softened, and with great courtesy he spoke slowly and simply, interjecting English often to keep me on track.

Highway 1 is the primary road that travels the length of this magic peninsula, beginning at Tijuana and crisscrossing from the Pacific Ocean to the Sea of Cortez until reaching the cape at Cabo San Lucas. The pavement was twenty-five years old, narrow, and without shoulders, leaving the edges subject to crumbling. Along many stretches, Jon kept the truck straddling the centerline, ready to dodge right or left to avoid treacherous potholes or encroaching cracks along the edges. We noticed the truck drivers doing the same thing, and he engaged in more than one episode of "Chicken" to see who would slide back into his respective lane first. Our first day of driving was a combination of high alert, sheer terror, and pure magic.

Our first fuel stop in Baja was in Lazaro Cardenas. At that time, fuel was sold at PEMEX stations owned exclusively by the Mexican government, and only employees were allowed to pump the gas. Again, we noticed that, when I spoke to the young attendant in Spanish, patching words together like "fill it up" and "receipt, please," he seemed pleased with my effort to try Spanish—even though I undoubtedly slaughtered the language. We both enjoyed the exchange and came away smiling. He was probably laughing at my bumbling, but my courage was bolstered.

Since our first year of making this trip in 1996, we have developed a few basic rules for traveling in Baja. Do not linger in the cities along the border. Do not carry drugs or firearms. Do not drive at night. Do not camp alone.

On this first day out, we kept them all— except one, which would be the one we broke most frequently. South of San Quintin and before dark, we followed Jon's nose off the pavement down a dirt road to a secluded overlook of the ocean. This meant there were no other campers around us, but we found it too irresistible to pass up. From that bluff, we hiked down to water's edge, where we played tag with the ocean waves and watched the sun go down. As night fell, the moon reflected on the dark ocean depths, a sea lion barked faintly in the distance, and we expected the sound of the ocean to lull us to sleep. Instead, the waves seemed to get louder all through the night, roaring toward us like a fleet of B52 bombers. Neither of us slept well because of the unaccustomed sounds of the

Our first campsite in Baja in 1996, on the Pacific Ocean south of San Quintin.

ocean beating against the cobble beach, so we dubbed this place "Bomber Beach."

Groggily, we raised our heads from our pillows as the rising sun brightly caught the high-reaching waves breaking toward shore. Over a steaming cup of coffee, I began to anticipate the possibilities of the day before us. Traveling in this foreign country made me feel anxious, unsettled, unsure. Unfamiliar roads, unpracticed language, unscripted travel plans—all were elements of a general unease. My instinctive tendency to seek joy rather than fear pulled me into a meditation about the beauty before me, and a Psalm seeped into my consciousness.

If I take the wings of the morning
And settle at the farthest limit of the sea,
Even there Your hand shall lead me,
And Your right hand shall hold me fast.

Along with Jon's expansive gusto for this adventure, the words of the Psalm quelled my jitters and brought a big sigh to my heart. Feelings of wonder and gratitude washed over me with the power of the ocean waves. A childlike trust nudged me on into the day.

After our first day's glimpse at northern Baja's agricultural zone, our second day took us through the arid desert section down the middle of the peninsula and east across to the Sea of Cortez. Our jaws dropped as we traveled through the Valle de los Cirios (Valley of the Cirios). *Cirios* are plants straight out of Dr. Seuss. Another name for them is "boojum tree," which generates an apt visual of these comic cacti. The Spanish word *cirio* means taper, like the tall wax candles of the missions. Initially the plants grow straight up, tapering at the top, and when they bloom, the little yellow blooms mimic the light at the end of the candle. Often the trees branch out at the top, veering off in odd directions, curling, angling, and gesturing in ways that are unimaginable and absent-minded. Stems and thin leaves along the trunk come and go with the rainfall. Leaves turn yellow and fall during dry spells, but new leaves sprout within seventy-two hours after a rain. This area of Baja is the only place on the planet where these highly adapted desert trees grow natively.

Another fascinating cactus species we found amusing was the *datilillo*, or tree yucca, sometimes confused with the Joshua tree of the southern California and Arizona deserts. The lance-

Cirio cacti, or boojum trees, living up to their name.

like leaves are perched precariously on top of the tree trunk, like a thorny and unforgiving bottlebrush. Like many other desert plants, the datilillo, or "little date," has a variety of uses. A medicinal tea is made from the flower buds, candies come from the flowers, soap is derived from the rootstock, and the fibers are used to make sandals. The datilillo is a smart and dependable plant rather than the wild and undisciplined teenager it appears to be.

Guerrero Negro is the town on the Pacific Ocean that launches Highway 1 across the peninsula to the Sea of Cortez. With our sights set on Santa Rosalia and moving fast, we made mental notes of the places to investigate on our return trip north, places like Scammon's Lagoon, the Sierra San Francisco ancient cave paintings, and San Ignacio, the gateway to whale watching at San Ignacio Lagoon. The pavement along this stretch was equally as challenging, providing Jon more practice in dodging potholes and trucks. Our second day ended on the Sea of Cortez at San Lucas Cove, south of Santa Rosalia, where we collapsed into the sunset and dreamed of cirio cactus and potholes.

Travels through the southern sector of the peninsula gave us a look at La Paz, a lovely, thoroughly Mexican city that curls around the Bahía de La Paz and throbs with commerce from its excellent seaport. This is where Jon had flown for deep-sea fishing trips before we were married. I had joined him one winter for a long weekend spent on a sailboat he was tending out in the bay. Perhaps those trips were the spark that ignited this great

love affair we have with Baja. In later years, La Paz would draw us back often for a taste of real Mexico, with its *mercados* and *malecón*—markets and waterfront promenade—teeming with the flavors, colors, music, and sounds of day-to-day life that we love.

Further south, all the way to the cape, we were bombarded by another kind of commerce in the town of Cabo San Lucas, an Americanized tourist hot spot. The coast is lined with high-rise waterfront hotels, resorts, golf courses, restaurants, and gift shops that accommodate the tour ships and all-inclusive vacations of people from around the globe. We passed through the area quickly, looking for a less civilized place where we, and our little pop-up camper, would feel more at home.

Crossing back over to the Sea of Cortez, we found such a place south of La Paz at Bahía de los Muertos (Bay of the Dead). Protected from the north winds, the bay was quite popular for fishing, kayaking, and snorkeling. Watching the birds here became our primer for learning about sea-bird behavior. We had no idea that plummeting into the water as beak-first kamikaze pilots was normal. Why would a pelican do such a crazy thing? We watched their insanity time and again and felt like we were watching a circus. As it turns out, seabirds come to the dinner table in one of four different ways: surface feeding, pursuit diving, plunge diving, and/or scavenging. With the pelicans, we were observing plunge diving, a skill that might take a pelican many years to master and allows the bird to dive from as high as seventy feet to capture prey.

OPPOSITE, TOP *Datilillos* leaning into a rainbow.
MIDDLE Visions of cactus dancing under a full moon.
BOTTOM A traditional *mercado* (market) in downtown La Paz.

TOP Pelicans demonstrate the fine art of plunge diving for their dinner.
BOTTOM A blue-footed booby takes aim at breakfast.

Terns, boobies, and pelicans are among the seabirds in Baja that employ these table manners.

The least mannerly method of feeding we watched was scavenging, also called kleptoparasitism, a perfect word to describe this marine piracy. Sea gulls were the most frequent kleptos, although frigate birds and terns were not above stealing food from the full pouches of pelicans. Scavenging is only a second job for the birds that feed this way. Stealing food from others is a hard way to make a living.

At the Bahía de los Muertos, we also had our first glimpse into the challenges faced by the ranchers of Baja. A fellow camper we were just getting to know was fundamentally vegetarian, but one evening ended up eating chicken with us, due to an encounter with some hungry cows. He was preparing his evening supper, a salad made with tomatoes, avocados, and garbanzo beans, and topped with sprouts he had been growing. He walked away from the outdoor table for a brief moment, to come back to a couple of very skinny cows earnestly grazing at his salad bar. We have scratched our heads and wondered why ranchers even try to raise cattle in this harsh and unforgiving land of minimum rain, scarce vegetation, and unrelenting heat. No wonder those cows could smell fresh sprouts from a mile away.

Erratic as it is, cattle ranching has a rich tradition in Baja California. As a matter of fact, the cowboy heritage of America took its origins from the *Californios*, the Mexican *caballeros*. But

A tern heads home after a successful hunt.

like the cacti that populate the long expanse of this narrow strip of land, cattle are dependent upon rain for their welfare. Some years the cattle have plenty of vegetation to sustain them. During dry years, the years of the *sequía*, they shrink in size or number, or are completely wiped out. This was a year of the sequía.

After breaking camp and finding a small *tienda* (store) in Agua Amarga to buy avocados, potatoes, and tortillas, we continued down the coast road a few miles and turned toward the water on a very narrow dirt road. An incredibly beautiful beach came into view. We ended up spending two nights. The first morning before sunrise, we were out in our kayaks, catching the brilliant colors of sky and water as the sun pulled back the curtain of darkness. By day we snorkeled, kayaked, hiked, and marveled at how people seemed to have completely overlooked this lonely, lovely place. By night we listened to the waves splashing over our contentment and heard coyotes howling beneath our slumber.

Having sampled the delights of camping on the Sea of Cortez, we now made our way back around the cape, traveling up the Pacific side. Fifteen miles north of Cabo San Lucas, and with no clue where we would end up, we nosed our way out to a point overlooking the ocean. We found a nearly deserted beach with only one other vehicle in sight. I held my breath as we sought out a flat spot to call home for the night, and to my great relief, we did not get stuck in the sand. Here, we enjoyed long beach strolls both in the late afternoon and with the sunrise in the early morning. The next day was a repeat performance. Driving just a short four miles north, we discovered yet another unclaimed, heartbreakingly beautiful stretch of beach, unnamed as far as we could tell. We should have driven on to the next town, since we were almost out of food and dangerously low on beer, but this was a find we simply could not pass up.

The date was February 14. We settled in for a day of beach combing, wave dodging, and trying to put together a special Valentine's dinner. Knowing our food supply was depleted, we had to dig deep for that bit of romance, but even a pot of rice with green *chiles* can be romantic when it is all that is left, and you are where and with whom you want to be. Tomorrow would be soon enough to find a tienda. Today we were tucking away new memories. Realizing my initial travel jitters had subsided, Baja had become a tantalizing edge I was ready to continue exploring.

OPPOSITE A beach on the Pacific coast—made for beach combing, wave dodging, and dreaming.

images of baja

THE BAHÍA CONCEPCIÓN

chapter five

The further we crept along the primitive dirt road, the more entranced we became with what we saw. Now and then, we found evidence of a rustic fish camp surrounded by mounds of discarded scallop shells, but we were totally alone for the seven-mile exploration. Mountains loomed to the west. Even to the east between the bay and the sea, the gentle Sierra Los Gavilanes drew our eyes upward. Peering up those slopes and gazing west out at the glistening water, we kept wondering why this paradise remained so untouched. Why was no one else around?

We were on the east side of the Bahía Concepción—Conception Bay—a huge bay carved into the landscape from the Sea of Cortez between the towns of Mulegé and Loreto. This immense body of water is, for many travelers, the most beautiful place in Baja and becomes their annual winter destination. Twenty-five miles long, the bay is lined with more than fifty miles of beaches, many of which have easy access from the highway. Heading south from Mulegé, we caught the first view of its captivating, brilliant water, studded with islands and lined with beckoning white sand.

This year—our year of initiation, when everything was new, uninformed, and unplanned—we approached the Bahía from the south, headed toward the border and home. We did not know that twenty-five miles to the north was the most expansive and populated beach on the bay. We had no idea that the south end was rarely visited, so we did not realize we would be breaking the "do not camp alone" rule yet again. We just knew that as we left

An expansive view of the Bahía Concepción off the Sea of Cortez.

the pavement on the very southern extremity of this enormous bay, we could see an inviting sandy beach ahead with a private place to camp. I swallowed hard as the prickles of aloneness tried to undo the tranquility of the setting. I twisted the gold band on my finger and silently recited the words; "Wither thou goest, I will go."

We made this long stretch of isolation our home for three days, filling the hours with kayaking, shell searching, hiking, and embracing the brilliant colors of Baja's famous sunrises and sunsets. Jon even managed to get a little painting done while I had my nose in a book. On the third day, to keep from missing anything, we explored east around the southern edge of the bay and headed north toward another empty stretch of shoreline. Our intent was to check out this east side for future reference, and then backtrack to the highway and up toward the village of Mulegé for the night.

As often happens in Baja, we changed our minds again about going into town that day. We were captured, held hard by the beauty. Not far from last night's campsite and not making much progress toward a source of food and water, we gave in to the magnetism and found a flat spot to call home for the night. The next morning, we headed out in our kayaks to catch the sunrise from the water. Floating in the vermillion sea, I was engulfed in the assurance of our Creator's presence. The power of the throbbing red of dawn washed away my fear of that remote edge, replacing it with awe and wonder.

At breakfast, as I was planning a relaxing day of reading, Jon was studying the map, thinking more in terms of kayaking, hiking, and exploring. His contagious enthusiasm once again pulled me away from my books. With GPS in hand, he led us north in the kayaks, locating a place to leave the boats and begin hiking toward an out-of-the-way dot on the map. The dot was named San Ignacio and appeared to be a mile or two up the trail. Since our visit, we have always referred to it as "Baja Patty's Place." Patricia Lee Rentere, whose gravestone on site gives the name, was born in the 1920s. She spent most of her life stateside, living in this *ranchito* for the last few years of life until she died in 1991. The rudimentary thatched-roof *palapa* was closed off by a high chain-link fence and surrounded by rows of seashells bleaching in the sun. Nearby was a canyon that supplied water from a trickling spring. We were filled with questions about the woman who lived this remote life in an

TOP One of our new red kayaks waiting on the shore of the Bahía Concepción.
BOTTOM A vermillion sea at sunrise on the east side of the bay.

unlikely location, cut off from any semblance of community or ease. One legend speaks of a diagnosis of cancer in the states, a last-wish trip to Baja, a mystical healing, and her final ten years spent surrounded by nature's beauty in what must have been, for her, a sacred place.

After hiking back to the kayaks and beginning the long paddle south to camp, we saw a pod of dolphins out in the cove. With video camera in hand, Jon chased after them with his characteristic determination, set on getting video footage of the encounter. He moved faster than I thought possible in a kayak and was able to get some excellent shots before they outdistanced him. This experience for Jon was similar to my morning in the vermillion water, an active moment of being close enough to the natural world to hear the Creator's whisper and to feel the mystery.

We made ourselves leave the next morning for Mulegé and our much-needed groceries. As we drove along the south shore going back toward the highway, we realized why this beach was not lined with campers. Today's north wind was blasting straight toward land with no possible protection from the elements. The water pounded deafeningly against the shingle beach and the wind pinned our ears back. We took note of the remnants of an abandoned RV Park near the road, which we learned was an attempt by the government to provide recreation for tourists. They just forgot to factor in the harsh environment when the north wind blows, which is often. Their dreams, like many other Baja schemes, just blew away.

Dolphins splashing in front of Jon's kayak.

This was only one of several facts we learned as we drove north, all proving that no paradise is without its pitfalls. Before reaching Mulegé, we were lured off the highway down another dirt road that led out to the sea. Why not check it out for next year? The detour ended at a rocky beach, again with no campers in sight. We assessed the area quickly as we walked down to the water and over to one end of the beach. Away from the camper for fifteen minutes, we arrived back to discover the vent window of the truck had been broken, our video camera with the dolphin footage was gone, and the fanny pack I had complacently left in sight was open, bloody and missing the pesos I kept there. Stunned, we followed the dirt road that meandered through the desert vegetation flanking the beach and discovered two other couples who had also been robbed. Thus began our day of cops and robbers.

In Mulegé, the six of us told our story to the comandante de policia (police chief), who then deputized all the friends he could round up—right down to pinning a star on their shirts. They were in no way equipped to drive to the scene of the crime, so they asked to borrow our vehicles, our binoculars, and our two-way radios to get to the beach. We all piled in and drove down together. Various guns appeared as the "posse," along with Jon and the other two male victims, headed on foot up the hill that borders the beach to the north, toward a cave that might be a hideout for the robbers. We three female victims remained with the vehicles, watching with binoculars and armed with radios, in case we needed to alert the men of anyone trying to run away from the cave. More than once, we looked at each other and laughed, wondering out loud if this really was happening. The posse did not unearth bad guys or loot, and as we drove back to town, all the law enforcers drank beer that we bought for them and then threw their beer cans out the window. Somehow, we felt as though we had just starred in a bad B-rated, old-timey western shoot-'em-up. With no shooting and no satisfaction.

People often ask us if we feel safe driving into Baja, and after a few years of experience, our answer is always the same. With this one rather benign and comic exception, we have had no problems with crime. We have had to deal with bribery on occasion, like paying the traffic cop 100 pesos ($10) for not wearing our seat belts. Panhandling will occur in any developing nation. We have been targeted as tourists with the attendant problems of clerks trying to short-change us or claim not to have change at all. But cheating is a part of life, and crime can and does happen as easily in Lawrence, Kansas, as in La Paz, Baja California Sur.

In 2009, we found ourselves in a maelstrom of bad press about the rise of crime in Mexico. We heard it on all sides. In our mad dash toward the sun, we felt uneasy about the prospects of traveling south of the border. Operating under the cloud of all that negative press, listening to the concerns of our family and friends, and feeling the constraints of a "down" economy and an aging motorhome, we reached Yuma, Arizona, with our minds made up. We were going to be sensible and not go to Baja. We would save money, be responsible, and not put ourselves at risk. Then we ran out of vanilla and tequila. Naturally, we had to resupply, so we just ran across the border at Algodones, the nearest crossing to Yuma, to buy the necessities and have lunch. That should satisfy our craving. We fought off the street vendors, bargained for our vanilla, found a great little out-of-the-way *mercado* and ordered up lunch. One taste of those *carne asada* street tacos, served up with the familiar ring of Spanish, and our little fix backfired, simply stirring up an addiction we were trying to hold at bay. That night, as we tossed and turned, trying to sleep, Jon finally nudged me fully awake with his classic line, "I have an idea." I knew what the next words would be. "Let's go to Baja," and within twenty-four hours, we were Baja-bound.

The economy would be what it would be, no matter what side of the border we were on. Ed, the motorhome, was not getting any younger, and neither were we. The media rants had served their purpose, reminding us to avoid border towns, stay far away from the drug scene, and never drive at night. We decided not to be ruled by fear. The Baja we know dwells deep within the heart of this country, where we see flashes of the America of our childhood—simple, undemanding, honest, and God-loving. Baja is not a perfect place, but, rather a place that continually brings us pleasure and draws us back. No one we knew was very surprised about our decision. Our friends and family were all aware of our addiction.

Since our first discovery of it, the Bahía Concepción on the Sea of Cortez has remained a touchstone for us as we find our way up or down the magic peninsula. One evening, after just arriving there to visit some friends, Jon jumped down from the camper onto the beach in the dark. As his feet hit the sand, shockwaves of blue sparkles shot through the nearby water. He jumped again, and as he landed, more tiny blue fireworks exploded in the dark sea. Walking closer to the shoreline, we noticed the same blue sparkles hitting the sand with each gentle wave. We were discovering the phenomenon of bioluminescence, which means the production and emission of light by a living organism. An algae bloom that is sometimes called Red Tide had spread through the bay, bringing with it phosphorescent plankton. The plankton will glow in response to movement, emitting color similar to a glow stick or firefly. The first

Bioluminescence on the bay of Playa los Cocos.

sparkles we saw were startled fish, reacting to the vibration of Jon's feet hitting the sand. We took our kayak paddles and caressed the surface of the water, laughing as the splashing water glimmered blue. We jumped in the kayaks and chased each other around, yipping and playing amidst the microbursts of color. A dog from the beach walked out into the water up to his neck, and when he walked out, he sparkled all over, except for his head, making him look like a blue headless creature from the black lagoon. Other campers joined in and by the end of the evening, we felt like we had been to a carnival.

The next morning's sun beckoned us out onto the water. We paddled over to one of the nearby islands, investigating all sides of it and settling onto a small beach for a picnic lunch. Jon clambered up a steep rocky hill for the best view, as is his habit, while I soaked up the sun's rays at water's edge, meditating on the beauty and contemplating the paddle back. As a novice kayaker, I was not happy to see the wind beginning to stir up the water with increasing fervor, ruffling up the previously calm surface. Since I am a desert rat, water, for me, is a foreign substance and a dangerous edge. Calm is okay. Rowdy is not. As Jon approached, ready to head back to camp, my heart sank when he instructed me to put on my kayaking spray skirt. Spray skirts were used only when it looked like we might get swamped.

Anxiously, I slid into the boat, pulled the spray skirt around, and with my heart pounding, faced the oncoming waves. Jon pushed me out, instructing me to paddle into the waves, not sideways to them, and then he came after. Suddenly, it seemed some force outside myself propelled me through the water. I heard my heart-song from the beach rise up within me, keeping me purposeful and unafraid. "In You, my Lord, I live and move and have my being. In me, My Lord, You live and move and have Your being." To Jon's amazement, he could not catch up with me until halfway across. When he could not see me in the troughs below the white caps ahead of him, he thought, "Man, I'll never get her back in a kayak again!" He was deeply relieved when he caught up with me—with a huge grin on my face. He grinned back, and we paddled toward shore in unison against the wind.

In 2014, we were in the familiar surroundings of the Bahía Concepción once again, visiting Pat and Jerry Harvey, who had been seeing whale sharks out in the bay in recent days. As they

TOP Sunbathing on an island before the wind came up.
BOTTOM Paddling close enough to the whale shark to touch it.

told us about them, our curiosity was piqued. Were they talking about a whale or a shark? Were they dangerous? Our friends set the record straight. Although they are big enough to be whales, they are actually fish—the largest fish ever to exist. As plankton eaters, they do not look at people as prey. Even with that information, I tried every ploy I could think of to avoid going out to see a creature associated with the word "shark." But my timidity was no match for Jon's determined zeal and our hostess's insistence. With rubber legs, I slid into the kayak and we set out toward those menacing dorsal fins.

I was simply not prepared for that close-up encounter. Measuring around thirty-five feet long, the mama whale shark seemed to welcome our company, shadowed by her twenty-five-foot-long baby. Slowly, dreamily, we floated together, drifting in wide, choreographed circles. We were in a borrowed tandem kayak, Jon in the front, camera ready, while I was the paddler in the back. He kept urging me to paddle closer. I gauged the distance and went as close as I thought safe. He shouted, "Closer. I want to touch the fin." I pushed us closer, feeling a bit leery about the power and sensitivity of this enormous creature. "Keep going," he insisted, and, with raised eyebrows, I finally, tentatively got him close enough to touch the fin. He laughed and proclaimed in surprise that it felt like sandpaper. In utter wonder, we moved through the water with the mother and her baby, all of us at ease but still on alert. Finally, when the little one seemed to tire of our presence, he dove under our boat, flicked his tail against the bottom, and sped away. We sat mesmerized, watching them go.

Our hosts, Pat and Jerry, own a home on one of the popular beaches on the Bahía. Their love affair with Baja had caused them to put down deep roots where they could absorb the culture, the community, and the generosity of this gentle people—and in turn, give something of themselves back. One year, they traveled with a church group on a mission trip south toward Agua Verde and out to the remote fishing village of Timbabiche, where they delivered food, clothing, and loving concern to the local population. On the boat ride back to Agua Verde, Jerry suffered a heart attack in one of the most remote regions of the peninsula. He was transported by private vehicle to the nearest medical facility in Ciudad Constitución. Miraculously, one of the mission trip participants was a former race-car driver and not afraid to tackle the treacherous Agua Verde road at impossibly high speeds. After being stabilized in Constitución, Jerry was transferred by ambulance to the larger city of La Paz to a modern and well-established hospital, where he underwent surgery. His report was glowing regarding the care he received. The medical team was skilled and yet warm and compassionate, even playing *salsa* tunes to lighten the atmosphere during recovery. He is sure he could not have had a better result anywhere in the world. After a few days, he and Pat took the public bus back to their house on the Bahía Concepción, with cherished memories of medical emergencies handled the Mexican way.

Inevitably, considering the law of averages, travelers exploring the same ribbon of highway for decades will have to deal with some mechanical problems or update vehicles. For seventeen of our Baja years, we entrusted our comings and goings to a twenty-five-foot Scottie motorhome named Ed, and Ed served us well. Named after the legendary environmental writer, Ed Abbey, this four-wheel drive, standard transmission, big-hearted, Dodge diesel rig endured unmatched washboard roads, endless *topes* (speed bumps), deep *vados* (dips), incessant military inspections, and the inside modifications of a creative artist in need of studio space. Ed muscled up when called upon to carry kayaks, extra water, solar panels, and mobile internet satellite systems. He even put up with the little tagalongs, of either the Yamaha Big Wheel hoisted up on his back bumper or Ruby, the Geo Tracker tow car clinging to the hitch behind. He gained character with each gouge, bump, or bruise, and flaunted the desert pin-striping left by spiky plants that designated him as a veteran Baja rig.

Deciding that 250,000 miles qualified Ed for retirement, we sent him off to a gentler life hauling a family of four out to local lakes to fish, swim, and enjoy the outdoors. As we thought of other options, I told Jon we should never consider a pickup camper because they were not built large enough to accommodate our lifestyle, which requires a studio, an office, and living quarters. But then I had never met the Bigfoot C1002 slide-out camper, either. With the extra space of a slide-out across one entire wall, we discovered the beginning of our new *casa redonda* (house on wheels). All we needed was a pickup to carry it. That was when Jon's brain switched into design mode. Actually, he had been dreaming of this design for a long time. We bought a Ford F-450 chassis cab diesel and had a flatbed built on it. Knowing that this truck required ultra-low sulfur diesel, and knowing that, at that time, such fuel was not to be found in the southern part of Baja, he also had an extra fuel tank installed to handle enough fuel to get down to our favorite beach and back. He bought a metal brake used to bend sheet metal and built several aluminum storage compartments that lined both the upper and lower sides of the flatbed. Four compartments were for food, including one with sliding shelves for cans and jars. Two compartments handled extra water tanks. One housed batteries to capture solar energy, one protected paper products, and yet another held his tools.

I watched in amazement as our "super RV" took shape. Once again I was stunned by Jon's ingenuity, which even found expression on the inside. He took the microwave out and, in its place, constructed five vertical drawers with shelves for spices, nuts, and canned goods. Every place he found a few wasted inches of space, he built and installed a drawer. Bookshelves, drawers for paints and brushes, and fruit holders he crafted with precision. I cannot begin to describe the tangle of wires, maze of solar connectivity, and plumbing parts Jon wove together to serve all his well-crafted plans.

As with all our vehicles, our new rig needed a name. After you have named one vehicle, you are then obligated to name every other one for the rest of your life. Otherwise, you would be picking favorites. When we took this new outfit to Baja for the first time, the name came to us on the beach. My focus for that winter was to release anxiety. One morning, as I was praying and contemplating the matter, a little head with big ears popped into my mind, grinning and saying, "What me, worry?" Alfred E. Newman of MAD magazine fame, my older brother's favorite reading material as a teenager, became my visual reminder to let go of stress and worry. Suddenly I knew our truck's name. I suggested the name of Al to Jon, explaining how just saying that name would make me laugh and help me release my worry. After thinking about it for a bit, he agreed, but for a different reason. His great-great grandfather was Alfred R. Waud, another artist who led an adventurous life during the American Civil War. He could see that connection as well.

Four winters of Baja travel in Al came and went without major vehicle problems, until we headed north back toward the states at the end of the fourth season. With our sights on the Bahía Concepción, Jon guided Al down to La Perla, a small, hidden beach with a few trees, very few campers, and a protected cove for kayaking. The next day, after a heart-stopping sunrise, we drove a few short miles up Highway 1 toward Playa Coyote, where we had plans to camp at our friends' home, also on the Bahía. Along the way, Al's message center flashed a warning. The computer message

Our new camper, Al, next to a *palapa* on Playa la Perla.

said our driving range was 500 miles before going to idle because of a low DEF level (Diesel Exhaust Fuel). Our initial panic involved wondering where we would find DEF, normally not available in Mexico. We also were aware that 500 miles would not get us out of Baja, and, since this exhaust system is not required in Mexico, few mechanics would know how to work on it.

Happily, we had friends returning north from the cape to the States, and through email, we were able to intercept them and ask for help. They agreed to look for DEF all along the way and were able to locate some in Ciudad Constitución. *¡Qué milágro!* (What a miracle!) They passed by the Bahía Concepción a couple of days later and dropped off the important additive. Like the good news / bad news saga, adding DEF did not solve our problem. The message still remained, indicating a sensor problem.

We knew we had to stop trying to solve the problem in the American way. We did try calling our Ford Service Department in

Rapid City, South Dakota, using the Wi-Fi cellular connection we created just for such emergencies. They were unable to help, saying since we were in Mexico, they could only refer us to a Mexican Customer Service telephone number. Speaking rapid-fire Spanish to this hesitant *gringa*, I believe the Mexican Customer Service Representative said they could have us towed to La Paz, where a Ford Service Department could help solve the problem. However, we had been told that the mechanics in La Paz were not familiar with this system and would be of no help. So, we purchased a "Good Sam's Roadside Assistance Plan" to come to the rescue, in case we needed to be towed, and kept thinking.

On one of his early morning beach walks, Jon ran into a friend of a friend who had heard of our exhaust system woes. He commented to Jon that a mechanic was coming from Loreto soon to help Juan Carlos, the owner of the restaurant across the highway, with some mechanical issues he was having. Perhaps he could help us, too. We hiked to the restaurant, discovered that Rafael, the mechanic, would actually be coming the next day, and he had an electronic kit he would bring with him. We described to Juan Carlos where we were staying, and he said Rafael would be able to find us. *No problema.*

Around noon the next day, Raffie appeared with his assistant, Sergio. I explained the problem, using the empty container of DEF to aid my limited vocabulary. He knew enough English and I knew enough Spanish for him to get the idea. He inspected the

Sunrise on Playa la Perla.

Jon captures the color of morning on an early beach walk at Playa Coyote.

engine, entered the Vehicle Identification Number into his hand-held electronic device which he plugged into the dash, poked some buttons, and unplugged the device, puzzled. Then he plugged the device back in a second time, scrolled up and down and back and forth, and finally proclaimed, like a magician, he was going to start the engine. He closed the door, cranked it up, and we all stared in disbelief at the dash. The dreaded message was gone. Raffie seemed as surprised as we were.

We all burst forth in hearty guffaws of relief, passed around high fives, and glanced furtively at the dash to be sure. Jon and I sang out in unison, "*Todo es posible en Baja!*"

chose that very moment to demonstrate the use of its blowhole, sending out a spray of what I imagined to be whale snot. Everyone in the boat was drenched, and Jon's photo of me with my hand poised to touch a whale tells a dripping tale. The baby probably thought we were impressed, and I am pretty sure I heard the mama whale snorting in laughter as they glided away.

The village of San Ignacio, which is the gateway for the whale-watching expeditions, is itself a quaint and dusty oasis that has beckoned us many times to stop for an overnight rest. The San Ignacio River runs through the *pueblo,* creating a fresh-water lagoon, along which dense date palms crowd the banks. Imagine the allure of an immense shady palm grove after driving for long hours through a sunbaked desert landscape.

San Ignacio is a prime example of what happened during and after the colonization and mission movements of early Baja. In 1532, a decade after his conquest of the Aztec nation on the mainland of Mexico, Spain's Hernan Cortes set his sights on what he thought was an island to the west of Mexico, across what became known as the Sea of Cortez. His early attempts to colonize the land failed miserably, due to the extreme conditions and the hostility of the indigenous people. In 1535, he landed in an area near La Paz and officially claimed the land for the King of Spain. Finally in 1539, Captain Francisco Ulloa discovered that this "island" was, in truth, a peninsula, and it became known as California. Still, no colonies were established and life remained much the same in this forgotten land.

OPPOSITE Waters of the lagoon reflect Ed, our motorhome, and the full moon.

The Jesuits, sent by the Catholic Church to win the souls of the indigenous people for Christ, were the next to attempt colonization. Thousands of years ago, the peninsula was first inhabited by populations of hunters and gatherers, similar to those in the Southwestern United States. The Cochimis inhabited the northern portion, the Guaycura were found in the central region, and from La Paz south to the cape, the Pericus were the primary inhabitants. In the harsh environment of the peninsula, the people had little on which to survive. The interior remains harsh, arid, and unfriendly, offering poverty of soil and a lack of water; however, abundant sea life is found around the edges. In days past, inhabitants supplemented their main dish with a diet of seeds, berries, edible plants, roots, and insects. Their daylight hours were spent simply surviving, as the people chiseled out a subsistence amid the cactus, rocks, and unrelenting heat.

Today, the peninsula can still be daunting and desolate. Hundreds of years ago, life was as basic as it could possibly be. Ancient ones wore no clothing and built no dwellings, making evidence of them scarce. Desert wanderers like us occasionally find *manos* and *metates,* which are the stones used for grinding dried seeds and grain into flour, but cave paintings are the most graphic records of a most intriguing life. It was a life that was destined to change.

Padre Eusebio Francisco Kino was the first Jesuit to arrive, living with the native population in San Bruno, near Loreto. Padre Juan Maria Salvatierra followed after him, and in 1697, he received

OPPOSITE, TOP Gail is inches away from her first touch of a gray whale.
MIDDLE Ooops! Missed her chance. The baby whale decided to spray his hello.
BOTTOM One bad hair day at San Ignacio Lagoon.

royal authorization from the king of Spain to found the first mission in Loreto. Though the Spanish military had been unable to prevail against the adverse conditions of this barren peninsula, the Spanish crown still saw a potential benefit in colonizing California.

Although the Spanish government stood to benefit from the labors of the Society of Jesus, it refused to fund them. Supported only by funds they could raise on their own and a few mission guards they had enlisted at their own expense, the fathers set about to feed, care for, educate, protect, and bring into the fold of the church a band of indigenous people resistant to change. The Jesuits subsequently founded eighteen missions in all, one of which was Misión San Ignacio, but their efforts were plagued with difficulties. They worked tirelessly and with great affection, but the incessant lack of water, epidemics of diseases brought over by the Europeans, and the natives' strong resistance to change led to an eventual collapse of the entire mission movement. Who would want to wear shoes after being barefoot since birth? How hard would it be to live confined in the close quarters of a settlement, as required by the priests, after having known freedom of place and movement? Trying to move hunters and gatherers into an agriculture-based existence with an entirely different value system proved more difficult than anyone might have imagined. Monogamy did not make sense to them, either.

The mission movement received its fatal blow when, in 1767, all Jesuits were expelled from New Spain, of which Baja was a part. At the height of its power and fame worldwide, the Society of

Jesus had created a threat against Carlos III of Spain, who issued a mandate for their expulsion from his dominions in Europe, Asia, and America. Their enormous investment in the advancement of the people of Baja vanished in a flash. The Jesuits were replaced first by the Franciscan order, and then the Dominicans, but their efforts were unsubstantial, and the land seemed, once again, to be unconquerable. Baja remained its stubborn, wild self and tried to forget. As if in a daze, the indigenous population—which had been reduced in number by European diseases—along with a diverse assortment of Europeans drawn to this unknown and mysterious land, put their labors into ranching, mining, and fishing. Tentatively, life moved forward—along with seeds of the Catholic religion, which despite all else had been planted.

The town of San Ignacio developed around a mission founded in 1728 by a Jesuit priest. The first buildings were rudimentary stick huts and adobe buildings. The beautiful Moorish-motif structure that came later and is now the centerpiece of the town was completed in 1786 under a Dominican priest and was named Misión Nuestro Señor San Ignacio de Kadakaamán. Of all the missions that were built in Baja, San Ignacio is one of only three original structures that still remain as a functioning church. Although the land was productive—supplying such necessities as figs, olives, pomegranates, dates, sugarcane, and wine—European diseases finally decimated the local indigenous population, which died out completely by 1840. The mission was abandoned,

Misión Nuestro Señor San Ignacio de Kadakaamán, the heartbeat of the village.

but the village held its own, providing refuge for weary travelers in need of a sheltering oasis.

Walking around the village of San Ignacio, we could easily see why the padres of long ago selected this location for a mission. Fresh water and the surrounding terrain suitable for crops were strong draws. We especially enjoyed camping next to the little lake, dwarfed by the towering date palms, and watching the birds that floated or flew by. Dates from the trees are in great supply, available for purchase all around town. The mission stands guard over the town square that is lined with a few humble shops and anchored with benches where locals chat over coffee.

San Ignacio represents a place of acceptance and grace for me. Jon's natural rhythm includes feet on the floor between 5 and 6 a.m., and head back on the pillow between 9 and 10 p.m. As a young schoolteacher and mother, I forced myself into that early-morning drill out of necessity, and my youth gave me the means to adapt. Throughout my life, though, I have always been inclined to squeeze the last bit out of the day, giving up activity for bed reluctantly. My muse loves to dance at night.

The difference in our rhythms is most pronounced while traveling in the small space of an RV. Jon's muse is all about the alluring colors and sights of the dawn. That is when mine is resting up from her late-night reading, writing, or crafting. The benefit of traveling in a small motorhome was Jon's ability to leave me sleeping while he slid behind the steering wheel and made tracks into the sunrise. But traveling in Baja was a different story. The only safe place while traveling Baja roads is upright behind a seat belt, and I did not want to miss any of the newness, either. For a number of years, I kept his pace, and even when we were camped, I would follow him out the door to greet the sun.

One year, camped on the San Ignacio Lagoon, Jon was determined to hike up onto the plateau overlooking the square to catch the sun's first kiss of the sleepy town.The image burned into his imagination and long before dawn, he was ready to go. My need to remain still that morning was stronger than his need to go, and I declined his invitation to join him. I knew I would enjoy the view through his photographs, and I knew I would revel in a quiet and contemplative start to my day. That began my guilt-free pattern of choosing my early morning moments, which became less frequent as time went by.

A favorite campsite under the palms in the village of San Ignacio.

Jon and the buzzards greet the day, overlooking San Ignacio.

We now laugh and say that Jon never misses a sunrise, and I never miss a sunset.

One night we will never forget was spent camping next to the lake in April, a little later than we are normally there. As the sun went down, bathing the lagoon with the husky tones of dusk, we began to hear the deep-throated notes of a resident bullfrog. No problem, we thought, as we tucked ourselves in for the night. We are going to sleep now, and our friendly serenade will end soon. Instead, the bullfrog brothers, cousins, and friends all joined in, and their full-throated concert lasted all through the night. We could not call a concierge. Earplugs were only mildly effective. By morning, we and all other campers along the water's edge had fled the scene, bleary-eyed and exhausted, with frog murder on our minds. We swore never to camp along that lagoon again, at least not during mating season, in April.

images of baja

CATAVIÑA

chapter seven

The first time we stopped to camp among the curious boulders near Cataviña, we found a little hideout only a short distance off the road, protected from the sight of other travelers. Tucked away amid the massive rocks surrounded by *cardón* cacti, *cirios*, and other thorny desert plants, we found boulders that had been hollowed out by nature, providing shelter for aboriginal people. Some were decorated with ancient drawings. We felt like kids on a treasure hunt as we climbed around the boulders, finding pictographs of a rabbit and a fish that a fellow traveler had told us about.

The Cataviña Boulder Fields stretch down the interior corridor of the Baja peninsula about 300 miles south of the border, between El Rosario and Guerrero Negro. They encompass the Parque Natural del Desierto Central de Baja California, giving them a protected status by the government. No matter where you are on the skinny Baja peninsula, you are usually not too far from the western edge along the Pacific, or the Sea of Cortez to the east. However, the Boulder Fields are totally removed from the sights, smells, and sounds of water. An official viewing site for rock art has been set aside very close to the village of Cataviña for easy access and education. Over the years, we have returned to explore this vast landscape—strewn with rocks the size of apartments, stacked one on top of the other, and decorated with numerous paintings. The place always elicits the same sense of awe and wonder we had when we saw that first rabbit and fish.

Can you find our camper, tucked in among the vast expanse of boulders in the Cataviña Boulder Fields? This is truly the middle of nowhere.

An ancient pictograph of a rabbit and a fish.

Boulder surfaces close to a highway also lend themselves to another kind of art— the graffiti sort. Many travelers do not bother to stop because of the messages projected by modern graffiti, which announce mischief under foot. One sort of mischief is conveyed in a selection of amorous symbols with hearts, arrows, and names of lovers. Bold, black Spanish expletives that we could not understand were something else. In all honesty, the graffiti, the distorted rock shapes, and the impenetrable silence of the Boulder Fields did cause me, the timid team member, much concern at the beginning. I felt an eeriness there that was unsettling, and I was reminded of the no-camping-alone rule. In one of the places we camped, we found a backpack that had been stolen and discarded in the weeds nearby. Finding it and returning it to its proper owner in the States did nothing to quell my anxieties. We heard rumors, as I am sure many others had, that at one time it was not a safe place, because of such thievery.

However, the fascination of the boulders, the beauty of the desert gardens, and the almost audible call of the voices of the long-distant past all lent magnetism to the craggy range that even I could not resist. I allowed myself to be drawn in, following Jon's confident lead, as we learned to camp well away from the highway in places hidden by rocks or trees. By focusing on the fantastic shapes of rock and cactus, my imagination was set free from worry and fear over who might be lurking behind the boulders with cans of spray paint or sticky fingers.

Jon having fun among the crazy boulder shapes.

A desert rock garden.

While hiking one afternoon through the boulders, we heard a truck driving toward us. To see other people roaming around was quite out of the ordinary, unusual enough that our immediate reaction was to hide. Instead, we held our course as two local men, Ismael and Pancho, stopped and introduced themselves. With great excitement, they told us to follow them, to see a new discovery they had just made. As we hesitated, they pointed to the identification tags pinned to their shirts, showing they worked for the La Pinta Hotel in Cataviña. They assured us they were good guys who had come to this area to gather *vigas*, or dried cactus beams, to use in constructing a cover over a porch at the hotel. The truck was indeed loaded with wood. Instinctively we felt their sincerity and followed them on foot to the end of the trail and further up into the rocks. Inside the shelter of a hollow boulder, they proudly showed us some pictographs even they had never seen before. They were elated by their new discovery, and we felt honored that they entrusted their find to us.

On another of our many stops in the Boulder Fields, Jon was out on an early morning hike when he ran into a gringo named Ralph, who, along with his wife Pat, lives in Cataviña during the winter months. They have fine-tuned the art of desert living. They also have a heart for helping others, and Ralph spends time every day checking on the travelers who camp at nearby Rancho Santa Inez, making himself available to help fix broken parts or locate other help as needed. He has assisted vast numbers of people

Ismael and Pancho share their new discovery among the boulders.

with a myriad of problems. "I had a few dues to pay from my misspent youth," he told us with a wink. Often on our journey up or down the peninsula, we stop to visit and catch up. Now in their eighties, Ralph and Pat determinedly tackle life every day with grit, gusto, and intelligence.

One year, Ralph invited us to trek out into the wilds to see a remote and little-known canyon where the walls are lined with petroglyphs. Unlike a pictograph that has been painted, a petroglyph is a picture that has been chipped into the stone. Our day with Ralph was like a petroglyph being chipped indelibly into our minds. We were on the road by 7:30 a.m. in his four-wheel drive Toyota pickup, pulling a spare four-wheeler as a back- up in case of emergency. The drive took three-and-a-half hours each way, and we spent four hours exploring the secret rugged canyon. As with so many adventures in Baja, we found a place of sheer wonder down a rugged, rocky, and primitive road. The canyon walls reverberated with story after story in a not-too-foreign language of pictures. We shared wild guesses, enjoying the speculation of what had been said symbolically here many hundreds or thousands of years ago. Later that night as I slept, the movie playing in my dreams flashed up images of owls, rainbows, and caterpillars all etched in stone.

Even as I found my anxieties quelled by the beauty surrounding me, I remained skeptical of the silence. In the Black Hills, we live apart from city sounds, but somehow silence in the Boulder Field is deeper, immeasurable, and impenetrable. At night, we would hear the distant call of a coyote, but nothing more. During the day, we often found relief from the quietness in the company of our avian neighbors, most notably the raven. No matter what boulders we chose to camp behind, a raven would welcome us with that distinctive croak, which no doubt meant, "Got food?"

Our good friends Randy and Jane Korb camped with us once under a rock formation we call Kissing Rocks, beneath the watchful gaze of The Sphinx. Jane had some fish she wanted to share with the raven, but she did not want to make it too easy for the bird. She knew he was a problem-solver, so she brought the fish out and placed it on top of a cactus with very long thorns. We all watched and waited, and within a short period of time, the raven's long and sturdy bill extricated the fish from the cactus for a lovely midday snack. We feel great respect for the tough birds, animals, and plants that can survive living in the Central Desert around Cataviña.

Petroglyphs symbolically tell stories of the people that came before.

We learned to respect the intelligence of the ravens so prevalent in Baja.

And when it comes to toughness in a desert, looks can be deceiving. Some plants are obviously tough, with thorns, thistles, and thick bark like the *torote* (elephant tree) or the *viejo* (old man cactus.) But at times I found myself caught completely off guard with the fragility of the fairy dusters exploding in miniature pink fireworks, or the soft and sumptuous nightshade blooms. The wicked *ocotillo*'s wiry barbed branches would, in its time, show off bright red, lipstick-colored blooms. Occasionally, sandy hillsides would dazzle onlookers with soft blankets of purple and pink verbena.

At times, walking through this unexpected rock garden, we would stop and gawk in wonder. How is it possible to find enchantment in the middle of the unrelenting reaches of a desert? What causes the fog to develop in such an arid locale? Why do blue palms still grow in the arroyos here, having disappeared from the mainland of Mexico?

And then there is the haunting question we have puzzled over year after year. How did these gigantic rocks become hollow? I gleaned the best explanation from a study by James L. Conca and George R. Rossman, entitled "Core Softening in Cavernously Weathered Tonalite." Not having a scientific bent, I can't begin to summarize their findings. They refer to tonalite, feldspars, biotites, and kaolinite, along with infiltration, dessication, matric suction, hydraulic conductivity, differential weathering rates, moisture flux, and geometric framework. My simple understanding is that when

A symbiotic relationship between the cactus and wild roses.

Fairy dusters proliferate in the arid climate of the boulder fields, despite their fragile appearance.

certain conditions cause the rock exterior to harden and the core interior to soften, the stage is set for the more rapid erosion of the interior. This "cavernous weathering" results in the magic Disneyland figures we crawl through, climb over, laugh at, and love.

Being overwhelmed with nature's mysteries disentangled my mind from my own timidity. Long hikes through the desert punctuated by nature's creative stone and thistle touches deepened my sense of oneness and intimacy with the Creator, and with those who had gone before. We lit candles in a roadside shrine deep in the heart of the boulders, allowing the flame to lift up our concerns and gratitude. We lost ourselves in imaginary play, seeing alligators, pigs, a sphinx, a dinosaur, all naturally and mysteriously crafted in stone. At the end of each day, we got goose bumps, holding hands as the sunset washed over giant boulders tumbling away in crimson chaos. My fear of this isolation eventually lost its tyranny, and, in listening for answers to mysteries, the silence became my cure.

Together we contemplate nature's silence, mysteries, and grandeur in the Cataviña Boulder Fields.

images of baja

SIERRA SAN FRANCISCO

chapter eight

At times, the Mystic Travelers' itinerary is planned. Usually though, our schedules and discoveries are totally serendipitous. In 2010, an unplanned side trip opened up a window into a world beyond our imagining. After spending most of our winter in southern Baja, we drove north on Mex 1 toward the border and began to see riotous fields of wildflowers along the way. Dense displays of yellow and pink were telling the story of the winter's rains. Jon desperately wanted to stop for photographs of this uncommon sight, but highway shoulders are as rare an occurrence as masses of wildflowers. Finally, we came upon a road that led east up into the Sierra San Francisco, an area we had always rushed by but never stopped to see. His idea was to turn off, snap a few photos, turn around and keep on going.

On the narrow road going up into the mountains, we found no shoulders or turn-offs and were forced to keep driving. Eventually, we found an even narrower side road, where we could turn around. We figured while we were there, we might as well explore, so we unhooked Ruby, the tow car, and continued east up the incline. We spent a couple of unplanned hours soaking in the sights of the mountains. The vistas were compelling and this mountain range shot to the top of our list of places to investigate more closely next year. We also knew that there we could find *pinturas rupestres*, or cave paintings, for which the mountains are well known.

The following year we were true to our conviction. We circled the village of San Francisco de la Sierra on the map, made

Gail saunters among an infrequent display of roadside flowers near the Sierra San Francisco.

arrangements in San Ignacio for a guide to meet us there, left the motorhome behind, and drove Ruby into the mountains. The way up to the village is one of the many deceptive roads in Baja that has been paved for a few kilometers but never completed. Ruby was used to the abuse of driving on gravel and therefore was not in shock when the pavement ended. When you hear or read the Mexican phrase "a good secondary road," expect several, if not all, of the following conditions: dirt, narrow, rough, steep, rocky, rutty, washboard, sandy, gouged with potholes, winding, dangerous drop-offs, no signs, and magnificent views. This was a Baja road.

Once in San Francisco de la Sierra, we wandered through the haphazard dusty trails of the village amid chickens, dogs, and excited children. After asking directions several times along the way, we located Enrique, the guide coordinator. Enrique called Ramon Arce, our designated guide, on his radio. Arce is the surname of a family that has lived in the mountains for nearly 250 years. Almost all the guides who give tours to the numerous cave paintings in the mountains are in some way connected to this family.

Ramon was well versed in the local treasures, and we set out to see Cueva El Ratón, or Cave of the Rat. He assured us that if we ever wanted to do the three-day mule ride down into the canyon to see the most famous cave paintings in Baja, he would be our man. He pointed out that clients provide all their own gear and food—for themselves as well as the guide, enough for three days. When I asked about his food preferences, he grinned and said he liked

A greeting committee of one welcoming us to the mountain town of San Francisco de la Sierra.

Chickens free range in the village.

traditional Mexican fare such as *burritos* or *carne asada* tacos, but he really loved peanut butter.

The ranch families that tend to these historic treasures take obvious pride in what they do. The site was protected with chain link fences and railings, and Ramon was an amiable guide. He showed us the *metates* (grinding stones) that had been found around the area, revealing evidence of the lifestyle of the indigenous people who told their stories by painting on rock. The dominant figures we saw were of deer, *borregos* (big horn sheep,) rabbits, mountain lions, and humans. One striking figure was of a human divided vertically, half painted in red and the other half in black. The colors were painted in fine vertical stripes rather than in solid paint. A black oval painted over the area where the face would be caught our attention. This is apparently a puzzling feature that is depicted in only a few of the rupestres of the area. We left the site enchanted by the mysteries.

In 2012, we ventured in search of new cave paintings, this time near Santa Marta, again in the Sierra San Francisco. Years back, a rancher, no doubt in the Arce family, had discovered these paintings while out rounding up his cattle. Having been assured that we could arrange a guided tour once we got to Santa Marta, we left Highway 1 at Ejido Alfredo V. Bonfil, looking for the "good secondary road." We had to ask schoolboys and the local police for directions to get out of town. Billowing dust behind us, we drove without mishap until encountering the low-hanging water line that

kept crisscrossing over the road. I had to jump out and use a kayak paddle to lift the line high enough for the motorhome to pass under unimpeded.

We discovered a simple but charming ranch at Santa Marta, complete with goats, peacocks (do you know how loud they are?), puppies, and a colorful flower garden. The guide coordinator arranged a tour for the next morning with Guadalupe. Looking at the roster of guides available, we were not sure if ours was Guadalupe Arce Ojeda, Guadalupe Arce Arce, or Guadalupe Ojeda Arce. The ranch's large side yard was our campsite for the night, and peacocks sang us their strident lullaby.

In the morning, escorted by one of the Guadalupes (we never really knew which one), we decided to hike up the mountain rather than to ride mules, making it easier for Jon to take photos along the way. High up, we stood dwarfed by pictographs that have been carbon dated to about 8500 years ago. As with the Cueva El Ratón, the display was impressive and well protected with railing. We were both grateful to see the custodial care given to the site and the pride the ranchers take in caring for it.

The Sierra San Francisco shelters one of the largest prehistoric rock art sites in the world. Our two expeditions into this unique artistic tradition gave a mere glimpse into the greater collection that can be found by venturing down steep canyons on mule back. The art has been well preserved due in large part to the dry climate and the inaccessibility of the sites. A management plan is in place to

OPPOSITE, TOP Gail talks to the guide, Ramon, in front of the Cueva el Ratón.
MIDDLE The features in this petroglyph elicit a few unanswered questions among students of the ancient *rupestres*.
BOTTOM A low-hanging water line was no match for Gail's kayak paddle.

A view of the cave paintings near Santa Marta reveals the size of the art.

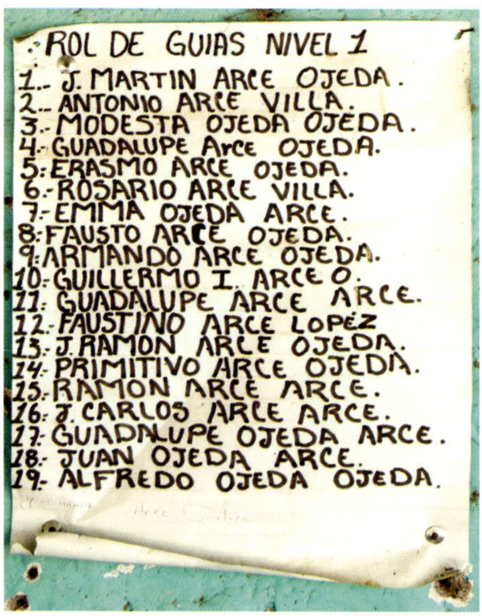

The list of *guias* (guides) who show cave paintings in the Santa Marta area.

protect this historic treasure, including being designated in 1993 as a UNESCO World Heritage Site because of its world-class rock art. Every year, we think about the idea of a three-day mule ride down a harrowing rocky trail to capture more of the magic of this mystical art. If we ever take the plunge, we'll ask for Ramon and take plenty of peanut butter.

TOP Driving Ruby down the mountain after our first visit, knowing we would return.

BOTTOM A long and narrow pictograph shows a running herd of animals.

images of baja

AGUA VERDE

chapter nine

After driving the roads of Baja for four years, we finally did it. We turned off on the bad road to Agua Verde. We had heard the tales about its dangers; we had heard the tales about its beauties. Nothing scares me off like rumors of risk; nothing entices Jon more than the allure of beauty. I had gone down enough bad roads with Jon to learn the truth of his philosophy: the greatest rewards are found at the end of the worst roads. So eventually, I was willing to concede to the bad part to get to the good part.

Tentatively, we turned onto the gravel road where the rusty sign pointed to Playas de Agua Verde. We reasoned (well, I *hoped*) that we could turn around if the going got too tough. However, turning around would rub against every determined thread in the fiber of Jon's being. We both knew that the thought comforted my less steely veneer.

The first eleven miles jolted our resolve with world-class washboard. When we would grind to a halt to regain our composure, the intrigue of the mountains coming into view pulled us forward again. The Sierra la Giganta is aptly named, as the giant rock escarpments lunge up majestically above the desert terrain in ponderous volcanic strata of green and red. Mesquite trees and *cardón* cactus line the stony roadside and spread in surprising density across the terrain leading up to the mountains. *Palo blanco* and *palo verde* give the landscape an African-savannah look, as if a faraway, wild grassland has been mysteriously planted here.

A view of the harrowing road down the hill leading down to Agua Verde.

A fellow traveler inches down the Agua Verde road, clinging to the cliff.

We picked up a couple of dusty teenage boys in cowboy hats who were hitchhiking back to their ranch after going to town for new boots. With courtesy and curiosity, they bounced along with us for two or three miles, no doubt wondering about these crazy gringos driving a motorhome down this road. They probably had seen few RVs in these parts, even small ones like ours. We let them out near a road sign announcing *Último Agua* (Last Water), where a house or two claimed what appeared to be the only, and last, water around. Reaching the plateau from which the road dropped precipitously down to the sea, we got out of the truck to try to assess what was ahead, the part that gave this road its bad name. We could see only glimpses of the gravel as it disappeared into creases of the mountain and slid into sloping shadows. Figuring we would never know until we tried, Jon shifted into low gear and crept down the single track, wondering what we would do if we met another vehicle. We kept our eyes on the large rock overhangs that pushed us toward the crumbling outside edge. No guardrails. Around each switchback, we held our breath. As we swayed and lurched over steep and rocky stretches, we listened to the jangle of silverware being tossed out of drawers jolted loose in the kitchen.

The moment came when I wanted to get out of the truck and walk—at what we later learned was known as "Hail Mary Curve"—willing to abandon my true love to perish alone if he tumbled off the mountain. However, if I had opened my door, my feet would have been suspended in air. Why had I agreed to this craziness? All

Gail opens the lemonade stand for the kids of Agua Verde.

Dolphins splash in the Agua Verde Bay.

I could do was to keep trying to breathe and pray, spinning my gold wedding band for comfort. I believe it is the first and only time that the perils of the road prevented Jon from whipping out his camera to take photos of stunning views.

Once we made the last turn and came to a stop at the bottom, we looked back up and cringed, knowing we would have to drive that same road back out. We drove another hour to the end of the road at the tiny fishing village of Agua Verde, where we settled in under a palm tree near the water's edge. One other couple from Alaska was staying in a pickup camper nearby, trailering a four-wheeler. Since we were just a short distance from the village, we soon became a source of curiosity for the locals. Our gringo neighbors established a rapport with the children by offering rides on their ATV after school. Rummaging through our camper for treats, we came up with peanut butter on crackers and lemonade, which we offered to the kids after their ATV rides. Toward suppertime, the moms would amble down to the beach to chat, often bringing gifts of homemade tortillas and fresh fish caught by their husbands. Eventually, everyone drifted home before dark. With no source of electricity, the village became pitch-black when the sun went down.

We stayed for a week in that idyllic place. It was the longest we had ever remained in one location. During the days, we wandered through the village, often in the company of community goats. We took our kayaks into green waters of the bay, for which the town is named, often in the company of a pod of dolphins. We

A vermillion sunrise dazzles the sky.

hiked into the surrounding hills, looking for the most expansive views, binoculars in hand for new bird sightings. Underlying the captivating activity, the specter of the hill we had to take on still loomed large in my imagination.

Early one morning before daylight, we heard a few surprising raindrops and decided it was time to go—before rain added another layer to our angst. Folding, cranking, stowing, and stashing in record time, at first light we tiptoed up that hill like guilty teenagers climbing stairs after staying out all night. As we began the climb up, I worried about the rain, which never materialized. I worried about cars that might be coming the other way and how we would pass, but it was too early for others to be about. I held my breath as we inched past jutting rock outcroppings, but nothing scraped. I gasped for air as we crested the mountain at the same moment sun splashed out of the sea, drenching the horizon in vermillion.

From the throbbing panorama at the top to the warm hearts of the people below, we felt as if we had indeed fallen into brand new and irresistible teenage love.

Not all our adventures involved just the two of us. One year, we had the good fortune of traveling with our tag-along, Paula. We called her Elmerita because she stuck to us like Elmer's Glue. Not that we knew enough about Baja to be guides, but we knew more than she did. So she followed. She drove a small 1978 Class C Dodge motorhome dubbed Harriet, and inside she carried some tools of her trade. We had become acquainted with Paula in Hill City, where she worked as a massage therapist, and on this trip she brought along her portable massage table.

On our first day in Baja, she fixed dinner for us as the sun went down on the Pacific. I was just getting to know Paula and was impressed not only with her cooking, but also with her kind and caring spirit. I was touched by the comment she made about our surroundings. "This is surely a place where you can still see God's signature."

For six weeks, we drove in tandem down and back up the peninsula, sharing the magic and dodging the hazards together. She hit one pothole hard and knocked out her power steering, but Jon found a piece of wire by the side of the road that worked perfectly for putting it back together. She was almost broadsided down near the cape when she flicked on her turn signal to turn left on the highway, not understanding that a left turn signal on the highway means "You're clear to pass. Go ahead around me now." The driver

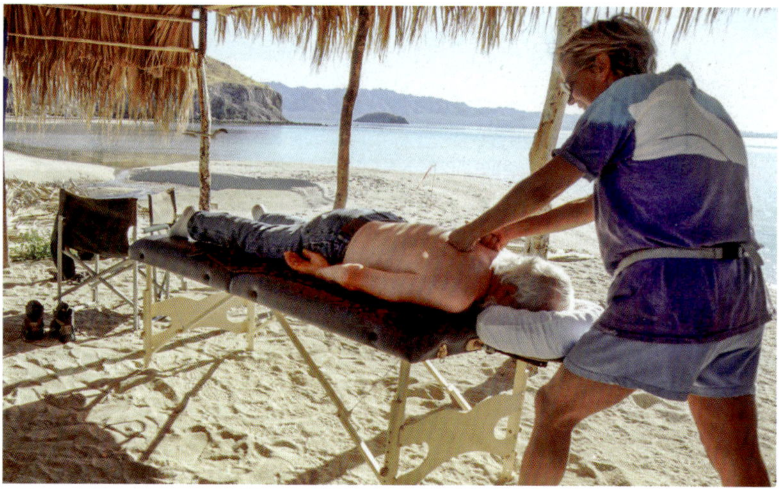

Paula, a.k.a. Elmerita, soothes Jon's tired muscles after a long day of driving.

behind her began to pass as she began to turn. Luckily, he had the presence of mind to go with her turn and ended up in the desert.

We kayaked together, and she gave us massages. We hiked together, and she gave us massages. We beachcombed together, and she gave us massages. She even gave me my first ever yoga instruction. Then, cruising along Highway 1 toward the end of our time in Baja, we approached the turnoff to Agua Verde. We knew two things. *Chubascos* (hurricanes) had come through since we were last on that road, potentially making it impassable for our little motorhomes. We also knew we could drive eleven miles to the brink of the dropdown to the sea, and there, study the road conditions further down. If it looked too bad, we could camp at the top. We decided to at least check it out.

When we reached the brink, Elmerita and Jon rumbled down the hill toward the sea on Dirty Harry, our trusty, dusty

1987 Yamaha Big Wheel. They came back shaking their heads. The chubascos had done too much damage, so we would stay put. The mountains surrounded us, charmed us, and held us for two nights. Clouds moved in and provided a moody backdrop for the sunset the first night. We clamored up a nearby hill, *piña coladas* in hand, to soak in the colors and declare the hill's forever name, Piña Colada Hill. The lush desert vegetation, absolute silence, distant view of the sea, along with the embrace of the ancient stone giants, provided a Baja memory to cherish as we moved reluctantly north.

A few years later, we decided to hazard the harrowing hill, once again winding our way down to Puerto Agua Verde. This visit conjured up images of what life was like in our own American neighborhoods a hundred years ago. We still saw no power lines and heard no phones ringing. The livelihood of the tight-knit community was based on a single commodity. Men went out fishing every day and women took care of the home and children. The fishermen had a communal system of counting and chilling the catch and transporting it to the closest markets, either in Ciudad Constitución or Loreto. Teachers came during the week from larger towns, arriving Monday morning and leaving Friday after lunch. They had sleeping quarters attached to the school and ate their meals in the homes of the children they taught.

We met the teachers inadvertently as we arrived in the dark, needing help finding the road to the beach, which had been changed by hurricanes since we were last there. A man drove by, asked to

Ed and Harriet camping at the base of the Sierra Giganta.

help, and agreed to guide us to the beach. As we followed him, another vehicle fell in behind us, making us more than a little nervous, especially when we were being led in what seemed to be the wrong direction. As our anxiety built, the lead car eventually swung back around toward the water, and we breathed a sigh of relief when the familiar palm trees came into view. The men in the two cars introduced themselves as teachers in the village. They invited us to come to the school if we needed anything during our stay.

Interacting with teachers and school kids became a highlight of both this visit and the next. The teacher learned that Jon was an artist and invited him to do a painting demonstration for a class, which Jon gladly did the following day. We invited the youngsters to come to our motorhome to watch Jon continue painting in his studio-on-wheels. Some days, a dozen or more inquisitive kids hung out, snacking on our peanut butter crackers and lemonade and watching the artist at work. They brought treasures to us in the form of shells and sea creatures, some of which were still alive. After the children left, we would secretly slip the live ones into a bucket of water and rush them back to the sea.

In 2007, we came again, just like the returning boats sheltered in the beautiful green waters of Bahía Agua Verde. As before, we interacted with the school, bringing supplies and equipment we thought would be useful in updating their technology. When school kids came to our camp to visit in the afternoon, we supplied them with large plastic garbage bags to fill with hurricane-blown trash from the beach. Then we would give them snacks. And this year, we brought a surprise.

Before leaving the States, we had planned a treat for the children of Agua Verde—white T-shirts in various sizes, along with iron-on decals. As the students came and went through the days, Jon took their pictures and transferred them to the decals. We ironed them on to the T-shirts and sent each one home with a new shirt sporting his or her photo on the front. Mothers and grandmothers made their way to our door, wanting to get all the children in the village in on the gift. We were not prepared with enough shirts for the preschoolers, but Jon did make sure to print paper photos for anyone who came asking.

I enjoyed a deepening relationship with Alma, one of the women from the village, who was married to Alberto, a fisherman, and who had two daughters and a son. Each time we returned to

Kids of Agua Verde amused by Jon's attempts to speak Spanish.

Three of the school kids sporting their new T-shirts.

had decided to pave the first ten kilometers (about six miles) of the road heading toward Agua Verde. The six-mile *desviación* (detour) around the construction was *muy, muy feo*, and at times we thought we would not be able to continue on. At one point, we encountered a large cardón cactus whose thick branch prevented our passing. As Jon began trying to shovel out a detour around the detour, we noticed a young man walking down the road toward us, rifle in hand. He offered to help, and Jon relinquished the shovel. Salvador was his name, which means deliverer, and that day he earned that name.

First he tried to widen the road with our shovel, an attempt that was futile against the unforgiving rock. Next, he asked for a machete, which we did not have, but we offered a hatchet instead. With that hatchet, he waged war against the offending arm of the cardón, whacking it off at the trunk and making room for Al to pass by. Salvador was no stranger to hard work. He took a few minutes to teach us about uses of the cardón, explaining that in times of drought, the ranchers will even cut up cardón pieces to feed the cattle and get through the hard times. Branches are dense with moisture necessary for life in the desert. Salvador became our deliverer, our teacher, and a good neighbor along this wild and, now, less intimidating path to the sea.

images of baja

SAN COSME

chapter ten

Sometimes Jon and I wonder why we cannot kick this habit of being beach bums in Baja. Why do we keep making the same trek year after year? In his *Log from the Sea of Cortez*, Steinbeck ponders this question: "If it were lush and rich, one could understand the pull, but it is fierce and hostile and sullen. The stone mountains pile up to the sky and there is little fresh water. But we know we must go back if we live, and we don't know why." We do know that no matter where else we might travel, we would always be searching for this peculiar combination on the Sea of Cortez. We would always long for this jumble of beach, mountains, and water, for the rugged gentleness of the people, and for the diversity of wildlife, sea life, and birds.

One of our buddies, Gary Steele, said he felt the draw most keenly in 2000. The rumors surrounding Y2K plagued him as he left Montana in December, and the unease followed him across the border into Mexico. The farther into Baja he got, however, the less it seemed that people were concerned. When he reached San Cosme, he asked the ranchers if they were worried. With no electricity or Internet capabilities, they had no concern at all. Doña Guadalupe told him she had her goats and plenty of firewood, and she needed nothing more. The Romeros invited him to church as one year slipped into the next. As he melted into the simplicity of their worship and their lives, he was deeply moved and, for the first time, felt relief from the worries of impending catastrophe.

Our Baja paradise offers the magic combination of beach, water, and mountains.

The sun rises on the Sea of Cortez, promising another day of unadorned beach life.

Stark simplicity is one of the tentacles that has held us captive on the edge of the Sea of Cortez. Camping on a beach two hours from town—and down a harrowing hill—forces uncluttered and frugal living. Once you get a camp set up, you want to stay a while, so you learn to make do. I confess to being a fussy girl, needing always to be color-coordinated and carefully coiffed. Hanging out in Baja with Jon, who simply does not worry about appearances, I began to learn the finer points of thimble bathing, hat camouflage for bad hair days, and shaking out my cleanest dirty shirt. Somehow I quit caring as much about having every hair in place and smelling like fabric softener or Dolce & Gabbana, but I will always have matching earrings for every outfit, even if I've worn that same shirt for a week. However, eye shadow became a hue of the past.

Water, propane, fresh veggies, and beer are the limiting factors that force us up the hill to town. Because we burn all paper trash and take edible kitchen scraps to the nearby rancher's pigs or the wandering goats, we have only small bags of recyclable items to tote to the *basura* (garbage dump) in town. My big splurge is having our laundry done at the *lavandería* on our visits to Loreto every two to three weeks.

In our first few years of dropping down that hill and out of sight, I carried a worried feeling with me to the sea, wondering how we would make do with our limited supplies of food and beverage. At Mystic, I learned I could not make a quick trip to the store if I forgot something for dinner, so I plan ahead and have a

The rising of the exquisite full moon.

huge pantry, two refrigerators, and two freezers. In Baja, I cannot run to the store on a whim, either, and campers do not have huge pantries or large refrigerators. Yet, at the end of two weeks, I realize that somehow food just happens and we always have plenty. Fish appears in plastic bags from our fishing neighbors. Happy-hour morsels sometimes substitute for well-planned and properly balanced meals. Using leftovers creatively and sharing shopping lists with neighbors make eating an adventure. Each year I experienced less angst and eventually found myself sinking deeper into the easy flow of unadorned beach life.

One Christmas Day, I reflected on the day's simplicity in my journal:

This morning, Christmas day, the celebration of the birth of Jesus, I walked down to the sea's edge to gather up water for cleaning the breakfast dishes. After I got my feet wet scooping up the bucket of sea water, I sat down to dry my sandals and contemplate the day.

Christmas on our Baja beach is outwardly a simpler day than it would be at home. Nothing much is scheduled, the ebb and flow of the day being languid and unfocused. We have no turkey dinner with green and red napkins, no elaborate planning, no over-muchness, no carol singing, no candlelight service, and no star atop a glittering Christmas tree. Where are my much-loved traditions? Where are the manger scenes and the piles of presents? How can I celebrate Christmas without them?

Down by the sea, I sat in prayer, asking how to celebrate without my traditional props. Amidst the wind and the waves, the word God brought was "cherish." The birth of Jesus among us was God's way of cherishing and calling His children to Himself. Rather than clinging to tradition, why not enter into what He was doing on that holy evening in the most humble of circumstances?

When my feet and sandals dried, I carried that word, along with my bucket of seawater, back to the camper to meditate and wash the dishes.

Tonight we will host a potluck for a few kindred spirits at our campsite, where we will celebrate Christmas and the fullness of the moon. The moonrise will be anticipated eagerly, possibly with wagers about the exact second or location of its appearance. No one will mention camels or wise men or gifts. No choirs will sing. We will light a campfire rather than candles. We will serve one

Singing around the campfire at Christmas, like so many other Baja nights.

another the humble offerings of a beach potluck rather than turkey and dressing and six homemade pies. We will share that moment of reverence and mystery as the exquisite full moon manifests itself and reflects upon the water. There will be music around the fire, along with stories and laughter, which will resound all the way up to the stars. We'll hug and whisper Merry Christmas as we part. Some hearts might listen into their pasts and hear a long-ago lullaby. Others will know a different truth. And God will be with us all by the sea, cherishing us, revealing Himself in beauty, and calling us to simple intimacy with each other.

We often try to describe to our friends what a typical day is like on our beach. Every morning we open our eyes to the diversity of the sea. Occasionally, the day includes winged madness off shore. Pelicans, cormorants, sea gulls, terns, and our beloved blue-footed boobies begin pouring into our little bay from the north and south, following huge schools of baitfish, and the orgy begins. We gawk in total astonishment as the birds dive, plunge, plummet, scramble, squawk, and elbow their way to the buffet, gorging themselves until they can hardly float or fly. The sound of the slaughter is deafening as open beaks and pouches crash into the sea. As it all ends, feathers float, bellies bulge, and we know we have witnessed a Sea of Cortez bird-feeding frenzy, or *picazón* as they call it in these parts.

Some days, the sea is like glass, and those are the days I choose to slide out in my kayak to explore. Jon enjoys challenging himself in big swells and choppy water as well, but not me. I go for glass. On one calm day, Jon and I paddled together to the nearby islands to the north. As we approached Isla San Cosme, a frigate bird delicately swooped down in front of our kayaks to scoop up his dinner in a single graceful ballet movement, barely skimming the water as he soared away with his prize. Although this seemed to happen in slow motion, Jon had no time to grab his camera for a photo. The moment is simply seared indelibly in our minds, in juxtaposition to the madness of the frenzied *picazónes.*

Inevitably, the winds or the tides or our moods ground us, and we turn to the mountains, arroyos, or beaches for our fun. In truth, I am happier on land. The more time I spend on the water, the easier it becomes. But she is always there, that terrified little West Texas girl who has heard too many stories and felt too keenly the power of the waves to ever be truly relaxed in or on water. Happily,

Winged madness during a feeding frenzy.

Kayaking on glassy water.

we have abundant options on land for hiking, bird watching, and beachcombing. Jon's photo library of birds bulges with the extravagance of images he has collected over the years. Our most frequent sightings in the trees include cardinals, Gila woodpeckers (alias squeaky toys), vermillion and gray flycatchers, mockingbirds, verdins, California quail, and pyrrhuloxia.

Occasionally, as we hike the road back toward camp, we hear the familiar call of the phainopepla, a shiny black bird with red eyes and a crest resembling a cardinal's. This is one bird call that we cannot mistake, and we often engage in a little back-and-forth twittering, sure that his "wurp" is an answer back to our whistled howdies. We have learned to identify the gray thrasher, as well as the Xantus's hummingbird, both endemic to the Baja peninsula.

The Romero family at Rancho San Cosme has mules and horses that they use to take people on expeditions along the coast or into the mountains. We resisted taking the mule rides for years because Jon's back has had its share of breaks, bumps, and bruises, and no longer tolerates jolts very well. But one of the years our friend Paula was with us on the beach, she and I decided we needed to go for a mule ride. The morning we chose was sunny and mild, and we had the good fortune of riding with Don Alejo Romero, the patriarch of the ranch. He has spent his entire life in this unique corner of the world and knows every inch of the coastline and mountain range surrounding his ranch. One of his *nietos* (grandsons) was going to guide us, until we both said we

I've walked miles and miles, I've got piles and piles,
But I gotta keep looking for more.

When I go down to Baja, I barely have time to do nothing.
Endless days of just watching the waves, but
I barely have time to do nothing.

When I'm under the ocean, I'm as happy as can be.
Whether it's an eel or a seafood meal,
There's always something to see in the sea.
The wind can blow for days and days. With enough books it just doesn't matter.
But today it's calm. I don't have time for a song.
I gotta get out on the water.

When I go down to Baja, I barely have time to do nothing.
I just wanna look and look, and maybe read a book, but
I barely have time to do nothing.

When I'm hiking the canyon, I've got my stick and my cap.
I'd like to take a shower before happy hour,
But I gotta have time for my nap.
When we're watching the sunset, the colors are starting to change.
Then the sun is long gone, but we're still going strong
And getting slightly deranged.

Jon's painting of Steve Smith, our beach musician, is entitled *I Barely Have Time to Do Nothing* (2015).

When I go down to Baja, I barely have time to do nothing.
I planned to stay, not lift a finger all day,
But I barely have time to do nothing.

Sometimes, friends will ask how we can possibly be content spending five or six months of the year confined together in the tiny space of a camper. Although most days in Baja are long and luxurious expanses of unplanned time, Jon and I find we get more accomplished creatively on the beach than at any other time of the year. Most mornings we are busy until lunch, with painting, writing, bookkeeping, or making rock and shell art; afternoons are for play. Celebrations come along now and then to add spice. For our wedding anniversary on March 5, we are usually still in Baja. We don't worry too much about gifts, but one year, we were hiking on our day, and I stumbled across a rock in the perfect shape of a heart. I snagged it, gave it to Jon with a kiss, and began a new tradition. He found the next heart rock, which was better than the first, and he became hooked, too. We now have hundreds of heart rocks scattered, piled, shelved, and lined up all over our house, not only from Baja, but from every place we travel. My ever-romantic husband has even conveyed love messages to me out of our collection of hearts. He once fashioned a big heart with my name spelled out in the middle for Valentine's Day; on our twenty-fifth wedding anniversary, he formed the number 25 with selected heart rocks outside our camper door.

One significant anniversary year was 2013, our 20th year of marriage. As we thought about how to honor the day, Jon tossed out the idea of renewing our vows, an idea I welcomed as if accepting his first wedding proposal once more. Again, I was challenged to look beyond tradition and realized that our chapel could be a rocky patch of beach by the sea, and the congregation could include pelicans and sea gulls. The music included "Give Yourself to Love" (Kate Wolf) and "Peaceful Easy Feeling" (Jack Tempchin), sung and accompanied by the guitar of our beach musician, Steve Smith. Pat Harvey, a retired minister and our trusted friend who lives with her husband, Jerry, on the Bahia Concepción, agreed to facilitate the celebration. And Jacqui Bonnifield added the perfect touch by wrapping us up in a fat blue rope and tying a knot, our Baja modification of a Mexican tradition. As the ceremony began, Jon looked at me with glistening

eyes and said, "You can't cry." I replied, "You can't, either." And we both did anyway.

As the ceremony gave way to hugging, dinner, dancing, and much merry-making, we knew we had just experienced something sacred. When I wrapped my arms around Jon, I caught sight of the now-scuffed wedding band on my finger and squeezed my eyes shut in deep gratitude. I meant the words inscribed in gold more fervently after twenty years than when we were first married. On that far-flung edge of the world, I realized I had learned to trust, and through that trust, I had learned to follow. Feeling the sand underfoot, hearing the laughter of our friends and the whispers of our Creator, we were cinched together a little tighter in nature's embrace.

OPPOSITE, TOP Jon's heart rock surprise on our twenty-fifth wedding anniversary. BOTTOM Pat Harvey facilitating the renewal of vows celebration on our twentieth wedding anniversary.

images of baja

SEASIDE MISADVENTURES

chapter eleven

When you camp in remote places with only a few other chums around, you share things—meals, pets, secrets, boats, misadventures, and sunsets. Sometimes you join together in contests like hermit-crab races, Scrabble, horseshoes, or bocce ball. Then there are times when you come together in rescue efforts, like the year of the lost yellow kayak. Shaunna, a fearless female friend, took her kayak out to go diving late one night under a full moon. When she surfaced after her dive, her kayak was gone. She swam a mile or so back to camp and urgently enlisted another friend to search the coastline. It was an unsuccessful effort. First thing in the morning, everyone came together to help. Jon took his 10x70 binoculars, the monster ones I always complained about tripping over in our motorhome, up to the top of a nearby hill. He spotted a microscopic dot out on the horizon and with radio in hand, directed our friend, Randy, in his boat, four miles out to the dot that was, in fact, the fugitive kayak. With the kayak safely towed back to camp, I sheepishly promised never to complain about those binoculars again.

Diver John, a friend we often camp with, also has an impressive story to tell. As his moniker implies, he is a dedicated diver who lives for the magic of spending time, eyeball-to-eyeball, with the fish. He is addicted to the feeling of floating weightless in the sea, the sight of sunbeams penetrating the depths, and the sense of kinship with underwater life. He asks who, as a child, did not want to be Peter Pan? Who could not love the innocence and

Shaunna and Randy rescuing the kayak that got away.

Diver John's beach camp.

guilelessness of a fish? Who could resist the enchantment of the sea's kaleidoscope of color and texture? Each winter since 2011, he has spent every possible day rubbing noses with the "reefies," or pelagic fish, and seeking the company of the curious predators in the Sea of Cortez. Diver John claims there is no such thing as an ugly fish, and his greatest joy has been learning how to relate to them.

Once, as he went out on a dive, he had hurried and, therefore, lacked attention to the details. As he made the slow descent toward his comfort level of sixty feet, he glanced over to his right, catching something shiny in his peripheral vision. Instinctively, he reached out to grab the shiny object, to find his entire set of keys in his extended hand. Stunned, he realized the keys had dropped out of his pocket as he made his entry into the water. In his haste, he had forgotten to leave them in his boat. Had he not caught them, they would have been buried in the sea bottom. They were the keys to his entire existence, including a camping van that sat locked on a rocky beach two hours away from civilization.

These things happen closer to home, too. I should not tell on my husband this way, but we've laughed about this story so many times that our history would be incomplete without it. In 2012, we gathered up our camping gear, cleared the kitchen counters in the motorhome, took down the mobile satellite, hooked up the tow car and left our seaside home. We headed north toward Loreto. Our first stop after climbing the breath-holding hill would be a water source, one and a half hours along the road to town. When we reached our

The set of keys that miraculously hung on as we bounced up the road.

destination, Jon could not find the keys to unlock the water tanks. His entire set of camper keys was missing. We looked in all the usual places once, made the rounds twice, and began to panic as we scrounged in every corner and unlikely place a third time. The last place Jon could remember having them was at our campsite back down the rough hill, where he had hooked up the tow car.

Dreading the drive down the horrifying hill again, but knowing we had no choice, he reluctantly circled the rig around and headed back toward the sea. As he drove and I prayed, an image emerged in my head of the keys resting on the front end of the Tracker, tucked in behind the bug deflector. I suggested he stop for one more look around. Expectantly, I rushed back to Ruby, and found nothing. With disappointment, we made one more pass around the rig. As Jon's eyes slid from the bug deflector down to the tow hitch, there, on the knuckle between Ruby and Ed, rested the prodigal keys. To this day, we cannot imagine how that precious cargo did not bounce off into the gravel, likely never to be seen again.

Rescue situations can build community, too, as we saw in 2013 at what is now known as "Crane's Corner." We had congratulated ourselves on an uneventful border crossing—celebrating the beginning of our winter season. We'd had an easy first night, nestled among the boulders at Cataviña, welcoming the assault on our senses of Baja's unique tangle of flora and the glad reunion with friends on the Bahía Concepción. We had cruised down the peninsula toward the Agua Verde turn-off, blithely wondering what kind of new adventures lay in store for us this year. At the top of the dreaded hill down to San Cosme, we unhooked Ruby, the tow car, for me to drive ahead of the motorhome, scouting out any damage the chubascos might have caused on the road since our departure last year.

I reached the bottom without a problem and was startled that Jon was not behind me. I waited, looked again, and still no motorhome. With my handheld radio, I asked, "Crane, where are you?" No answer. I waited, and again inquired, "Yoo-hoo, are you there?" Silence. Feeling a bit desperate, I asked a third time, and finally an answer came back. "Got trouble. Fell off. Come back." Flying back up the hill, I found him at the last curve, standing outside the motorhome, which hung on the edge of a twenty-foot drop off, teetering at an unnerving angle over the slope below. The road, which had been undercut by the storms, had collapsed on the outside edge, an edge my little Tracker had not touched. The front

Ed, the motorhome, waiting to be rescued from the edge.

tires and back bumper held Ed suspended across the chasm. The right rear tires rested on thin air.

No phone. No towing service down the street. Sun going down. We jumped into Ruby and shot out to our beach, looking for the only resource we knew—our friends. All the available men grabbed ropes, chains, and heavy vehicles, and headed back up the hill to the scene. Men from the nearby ranch came to offer solace, advice, and head-shaking—but in the end, we had to walk away that night like orphans, homeless and feeling helpless. Ed remained teetering throughout the night, leaving just enough room on the road for the few small vehicles coming by to pass. Friends offered a place to sleep, food, and warm clothing for the chilly night. We tried to talk our way into slumber, but sleep was impossible. And God offered ancient words of encouragement from the book of Isaiah: "You will not go out in haste, for the Lord will go before you, and the God of Israel will be your rear guard." I never before had a verse take on such a literal meaning with such a tangible promise. I clung to it like a life raft.

Julio, one of the young men from Rancho San Cosme, drove us into Loreto early in the morning to find a tow truck. The tow truck came, but could not help. Villagers from San Cosme showed up to support us with words, advice, ropes, reassuring presences, and coffee. Women invited me into the main ranch kitchen for tea to help calm my nerves. There I discovered that word had been sent out by radio to the surrounding ranches and eventually into Loreto, warning travelers not to drive down the Agua Verde Road that day, due to Ed's blocking the road. We had become famous.

The turning point came in the early afternoon when Rosabado came clamoring up the hill in a bulldozer. One of the men at the ranch had told him of our plight. As the man in charge of construction and maintenance at the big house on the hill, Rosabado had access to the D-6 Cat that was a match for our situation. He used the heavy machine to heave dirt out to the side opposite the chasm, widening the road to get by. He pushed and flattened a platform behind Ed from which to lift the rear end with chains between the trailer hitch and the bulldozer's blade. The tow truck driver offered his heavy straps, which the men wrapped around the motorhome and hooked to a *palo blanco* with come-along hoists. Slowly and carefully, inch-by-inch, Ed was lifted up by the bulldozer, pulled toward the hill with the come-alongs to prevent it from toppling down the canyon, until finally it was out of

The neighbor's bulldozer preparing to lift Ed away from the brink.

Having a *piñata* party to say *gracias* to our friends at San Cosme.

the ravine. Justo, one of the rancher's fearless sons, offered to drive it away from the yawning breach.

Before our "on-the-edge" experience, the big house on the hill had been a bit of a mystery to us. We actually complained about it, feeling it was an eyesore and out of place for the simple and rugged Baja experience we sought. Suddenly, I felt a great fondness for the mysterious house and its powerful machinery, and for the umpteenth time I found myself repeating a mantra that is hard to follow: "Never complain about anything—ever."

Jon and I both were overwhelmed with gratitude for all the rescue efforts on our behalf. Our beach neighborhood is not unlike our neighborhood at Mystic. We're like family. We've got each other's back. We keep trying to have a better grasp of the Spanish language to be truer neighbors to the locals who live here year-round, and graciously they attempt to improve their English, as well. We might not understand every word spoken by every person, and my Teflon brain does not easily hang on to new vocabulary words. But, thank goodness, you do not have to use words to communicate. After our cliff-hanging experience, we went over to the ranch at San Cosme to thank everyone in a tangible way for linking arms with us to get us off the edge. We, along with most of our beach buddies, ate dinner at their humble restaurant, bought jewelry the ranchers' wives make to sell, and then gave the kids a *piñata*. Eating together, making fun happen, and bringing light into the eyes of children seemed to say thank you better than words.

Sunrise on the Sierra Giganta behind our camp.

Don Carlon, also known as Gypsy Don, was inspired to write a song one year down on the beach, which gives voice to our experiences.

"The Baja Beach Bum's Lament"

We've all tried to explain why we come here
To our friends in the cold northern land.
We tell stories for hours in their nice ivory towers.
It's just something they can't understand.
They ask us,
"Why do you go down to Baja?
"What's there to do way down there?
"There's nothing around and you're so far from town.
"Tell me what's there to find way down there?"

Well, they've never seen the sunrise
With the Sierra Giganta behind,
Or floated in moonlight on a tranquil sea.
No, we're surely not out of our mind.

We show them all the pictures
And tell them it's better by far.
They say, "It's all true, such a beautiful view,
"But we'd have to get out of our car."
They ask us,
"Why do you go down to Baja,
"So far from the comforts of home?
"You're living outside, from the wind you can't hide,
"And there's no service from our cellular phone."

Well, they've never seen a dolphin's smile,
Or a ray flying free as can be.
They've never been swimming in a rainbow of life
Or eaten fish fresh from the Sea.

Our friends are polite and say it sounds nice.
We tell them we'll show them the way.
They hear our advice, but say they'll think twice
'Cause they have a big mortgage to pay.

Rainbow over the sea.

Coming back from a hike up the arroyo.

They ask us,
"Why do you go down to Baja,
"Fifty miles or more to the store?
"Wash your dishes in the sea, in the bushes you pee,
"And a shower's a gallon, no more?"

Well, they've never hiked up an arroyo
To see the great canyon behind,
Or lingered there in the cool, silent shade.
No, they just don't know how to unwind.

Now these days when folks they ask me,
I just smile and open a beer.
Baja's a dangerous zone. You're much safer at home,
'Cause we don't need a crowd way down here.
They still ask, "Why do you go down to Baja
"On roads that are narrow as hell,
"With washboards and dust, water you cannot trust?
"We honestly don't think you're well."

Well, they've never seen the pelicans dive
Or the feet of a Booby so blue.
They've never heard the osprey's sweet cry,
So don't tell me there's nothing to do.
No, don't tell me there's nothing to do.

"Have you ever heard an osprey's sweet cry?"

"Well, they've never seen the pelicans dive or the feet of a Booby so blue."

When our music makers are with us around a campfire, no matter how many times we have heard it, we beg them to sing this song again. Our heads nod in affirmation and our knowing chuckles add a deep accompaniment to the music.

images of baja

LORETO

chapter twelve

I thought that tiny year-and-a-half-old kitten was going to rip us all to shreds. Three grown adults—the vet, Jon, and I—spent thirty intense minutes cajoling, wrestling, and prying her out of corners where she hid from her pursuers. Finally, with towels and grim determination, we held her still long enough for the vet to inject the vaccine into the scruff of her neck. As we released her, Jon gathered her up into his scratched and bloodied arms like a baby, trying to calm and reassure her. She snuggled down in, eyes still wide and watchful, a growl still smoldering.

"Have you ever seen anything like that before?" I asked Dr. Dassia. She laughed and said, "Just remember, she is a Mexican cat, and she is a female."

Within our first week of being on the beach the year before, we received this most unexpected gift. Our friends Bruce and Celine, along with their son and his fiancée, had been tent-camping next to us and had spent their last day packing up to leave. In the night, this starving, five-month-old, orange-and-white tabby had strayed into camp and spent the night snuggled up outside the tent, right next to Celine's sleeping bag. In the morning, they fed her some fish morsels, gave her water, and brought her over to us.

"Listen, we can't take her with us, so here. All she needs is a little food and water. See ya' later. Gotta go."

My heart melted as I gazed into her huge, golden-green eyes. Here in Baja, they call a face like hers "*chiquillon*," meaning like a baby, and everyone on the beach was instantly in love. Our fishing

buddies donated fresh fish to feed her and doted on her like aunts and uncles. She quickly commandeered our camper, snuggling up next to Jon to sleep at night. Two nights after her arrival, we had a couple of friends over for dinner and began speculating about her name. Before the dishes were cleared away and the wine bottles emptied, we had agreed to call her Cosme, after the neighboring goat ranch, Rancho San Cosme. The next morning, Jon had a tiny, furry companion with a new name tripping after him as he traipsed down to the sea to welcome the sun.

Loreto, our closest source of food, water, propane, and laundry, now also became our source for veterinary care. The first vet visit was not much of a problem; Cosme was unsuspecting. She stayed overnight with Dr. Dassia, because we had her spayed and vaccinated, and she was still groggy when we picked her up the next day. We didn't think she would remember a thing. The following year, we discovered how wrong we were.

After realizing how averse she was to Dr. Dassia's office, we decided to try another vet in town for the rabies shot. He sneaked up on her in the new setting and before she knew to feel threatened, the shot was done. But again, the following year, she remembered that insult and the vet had to work very hard to corner her. As a matter of fact, he insisted we give her a sedative three hours before bringing her back in for the shot. We asked him to come out to the camper, which he gladly did, and although she was limp as a rag doll, she still had fire in her eyes. Jon, the vet, and I all worked in

OPPOSITE, TOP Our new kitten's eyes captivated us from the start.
MIDDLE Our new companion "helping" Jon with his painting.
BOTTOM Jon and Dr. Dassia grin while Cosme rumbles her complaints.

The pedestrian walkway that leads to the mission in Loreto.

The mountain mission of San Javier, west of Loreto.

concert to contain her, and he decided to give her all the shots at once rather than stagger them out over two weeks. For the next year, he suggested doubling the dose of the tranquilizer.

By the time Cosme adopted us, we had begun to feel at ease in the little pueblo of Loreto. Initially, our town runs would just take a day every couple of weeks. We would drop our laundry by the *lavandería*, fill our propane and water tanks, stop at several little *mercados* looking for all the grocery and beverage items on our list, have lunch at our favorite taco joint, and grab our clean laundry as we headed back to the beach before the sun went down. Buying fresh produce was always like a treasure hunt. I learned to substitute cabbage for romaine, chard for spinach, and *calabacitas* for zucchini. We became addicted to *bolillos* (hard rolls) and long skinny yams that became almost a dessert when roasted. I tried not to worry about the pounds we would inevitably put on from indulging in the fresh flour and corn tortillas from the local *tortillería*.

As time went by, we began to be a bit more leisurely on our town trips. We discovered a friendly RV park centrally located and often would stay one night as we made our rounds. We launched day trips from Loreto to explore local points of interest, including San Javier, a mission located up in the adjacent Sierra Giganta range. Our growing familiarity with the people, events, and attractions of the area made us want to linger and savor the flavors of the town.

This mobile way of living serves to accentuate life's challenges, maybe because everything is done in such a small space that is always

Gail at El Rey del Taco, a favorite stop in Loreto.

We never pass up a chance to buy oranges from the orange truck.

the owner if he could recommend a repair shop for Ruby's exhaust pipe problem. He sent us with a hand-drawn map to Antonio, who had a welding shop a few blocks away. We drove down an unpaved side street and found Antonio welding under a metal roof with no walls, no doors, and no signage. He stopped what he was doing, listened to our problem, and agreed to look at it *ahorita* (right now). Jon inched Ruby over an open pit and climbed down the wooden ladder to consult with Antonio. Together, they came up with a plan.

Antonio and his sidekick, Miguel, scrounged around the dirt floors, rummaged through the rusty refrigerator that served as a tool box, and rifled through a couple of derelict vans and pickups nearby to find all they needed to do the job. With patience and the experience of many years of labor, Antonio expertly resolved the problem. His bill was ridiculously low, so Jon paid him double. I thanked him profusely for working us into his schedule so quickly. He looked at me sincerely through wise eyes and opened up his servant's heart. He said we are here on this earth only for a short time, and with our one life, God prompts us to do acts of service for all people—children, grandparents, or strangers in our midst. And as we left, eyes damp, Alfredo's son, Frank, came by to check on his father and bring him coffee.

When we left Baja for the first time with a cat in tow, we wondered about our sanity. We had never really traveled with a cat before and knew we were facing new challenges. For three months, life on the beach had been free and easy for Cosme, with

Cosme and Toto take turns playing chase.

Tiny Cosme stalks the seagull.

unlimited playtime outside, plenty of lizards to chase, a couple of doting *gringos* who kept her food and water bowls full, and a safe place to sleep each night. She enjoyed exploring our neighbors' campsites, following us up and down the beach like a puppy, and drinking Jon's painting water attached to his palette. We laughed as we watched this tiny orange fluff ball stalk seagulls bigger than she was. We marveled at her instincts to hide when predatory osprey flew overhead. We applauded her abilities to discern when to have a standoff with a dog and when to climb a tree. One of our friends had a small but feisty dog named Toto, and the two would take turns playing chase.

Steve, the guitar player on the beach, nicknamed our kitten "Foxie Face," pointing out that her little emaciated face looked more like a fox than a cat. Her long, striped tail did not seem to fit her tiny body, and we wondered if she would ever grow to match its length. We spent hours watching her kitten antics, including chasing that long tail, diving under rugs to hide, bounding up trees to get the best view of the campsite—all the behaviors typical of kittens, but with a wild overlay. We speculated about how our hot-blooded Mexican kitten would adapt to the snows of South Dakota. Would northern mice entice her as much as southern lizards?

As we headed north toward the border in March 2015, we were nervous about going through customs with a cat, having never done it before, but we were prepared with her medical records showing she had been vaccinated. At the military check points

heading south, we are generally waved on through, but northbound vehicles warrant a search. We are used to having our cabinets opened in the camper and the glove compartment searched in the truck, as the uniformed youngsters with weapons look for drugs or guns. Cosme simply became a topic of conversation with the inspectors, who enjoyed finding out about our little Mexican rescue kitty. They were fascinated by her story and her name.

Still we were worried about the inspection at the border, where we are always sent to the secondary hold lot to be searched and interrogated. This year was no exception. To our great relief, the customs official was more concerned about our oranges, potatoes, and avocados than with our furry passenger. She asked about, and was riveted by, our kitten's story, but never asked for documents of any kind. Then she waved us through, wished us all well, and Cosme's new American adventure began.

OPPOSITE Rock art on the beach featuring a wild and curious cat.

images of the journey

SAUNTERING NORTH

chapter thirteen

In 1996, after our first venture down to Baja, I remember wanting to get out and kiss the soil when we crossed back into the States. Tentatively, we eased through the border town of Mexicali, proud of ourselves for being able to follow the signs and find the long line for the customs office. We had prepared to cross by eating any fruit or meat that would not be allowed into the States, such as oranges, apples, and chicken. We cooked eggs that, if raw, would be confiscated, and made guacamole out of the avocados, dispatching the seeds to the *basura* (garbage). The immigration officials were thorough and pleasant enough, but drug-sniffing dogs tended to cancel out a cordial welcome. Once the inspection was completed and our tires were on American soil, a deep sense of relief flooded over us, thanks to a renewed sense of safety and familiarity. Now, after crossing the border, repeatedly, for so many years, we barely notice a change, any more than we would notice crossing over from South Dakota to Wyoming.

Every year's meander north from the border is different, but our goals are the same. We seek time with family and friends, and we continue our search for beauty in nature. Jon's entire persona seeks beauty, which is why we find ourselves on the outer edges of all the places we go. His goal is to get to the top of the mountain for the best view. Keep pushing past good campsites to find the one that takes your breath away. Be present from the first glimmer of the sun's probing rays to evening's diamond benediction. The edges of the day are his obsession. And, so his quest for beauty has

As we travel, our quest is to be present to beauty from sunrise to the day's last bit of color.

become mine as well, and I stretch to the point of teetering, as long as it involves birds, rocks, shells, relationships, God moments, and some measure of safety.

Typically, our first stop after crossing the border is Yuma, Arizona, where tolerant friends provide shelter as we unload layers of sand and sea salt. We coax ourselves back into using a calendar and cell phones, and recount our endless tales of the charms of Mexico. Once we have removed all the thorns and tightened the camper's rattles, we settle on a route for the road home. The Phoenix area always factors in to start, where we catch up on the lives of family and friends, camping in a cul-de-sac, sharing pizza Fridays, lamenting family losses, and reveling in weddings and births. Cosme is of special interest to one of the family's youngest members, our great-niece Clare, who insists on visiting the camper to see our furry companion every time she comes to visit. Then we zigzag our way through the desert southwest, deepening our love affair with the canyons, deserts, and mountains of Arizona, Utah, Nevada, and California.

On this leg of the journey, we focus *not* on aspects that remind us we have crossed the border—fast food, elaborate truck stops, and signs in English—but instead on whatever erases the idea of borders. Cacti, tumbleweeds, the emptiness between cities. And birds. Always birds. I remember the exact moment when I became a bird-watching maniac. I stepped out the camper door at Catalina State Park in Arizona with my new binoculars and saw a beauty perched on a slender branch twenty feet away. Just learning to handle the binoculars, I managed to find the bird and bring it into focus. My world was transformed, and I could have been anywhere. I made out yellow eyes, a gray shape that was not a sparrow, and a fascinating bill that was long and curved downward. After staring speechless until he escaped my gaze, I grabbed my brand new *Field Guide to the Birds of North America* by National Geographic, riffled through the pages for a match, and made an entry: curve-billed thrasher – February 12, 2003.

I had been trying to get the hang of bird watching for about a year, borrowing Jon's binoculars to catch a few birds around home, including the mountain blue bird, the black-capped chickadee, and the American goldfinch. Why did the curve-billed thrasher send a jolt through my body, grab me hard, and drag me into the deep waters of addiction, binoculars dangling from my neck? Maybe I

was trying to justify the expense of a good pair of field glasses of my own and a good field guide. One symptom of my addiction became the compulsion to have my Minox 8x32s attached to me at all times, like a favorite and well-worn accessory.

However, as magical as birds are, even they could not make me into a morning person. Over the years, even Jon had quit trying to do that. When we traveled in Ed, the motorhome, we had a pass-through between the cab and the coach. Jon learned to his deep satisfaction that he could ease quietly into the driver's seat before dawn and cover many miles before I, the night owl, fluttered down to join him. To his amusement, I have missed entire states before opening my eyes. His greatest disappointment with our current camper, Al, is the absence of a pass-through between the camper and the truck's cab, which means he must wait until his sleepy copilot is dressed, fed, and in the cab before beginning the day's drive. He has undoubtedly missed a few sunrise photos because of my early morning ineptitude, and I'm sure I have missed spotting a few early-morning birds.

One year, driving through the southeast corner of Arizona, we discovered the Chiricahua Mountains, and in them, a bird-watching bonanza. Since then, every chance we get, we disappear into the craggy folds of isolated canyons and mountains, enslaved by the expectation of a new sighting. When we are there, we wear ourselves out hiking, searching, listening, and making notes in the field guide. Jon became as avid about the search as I, and part of the

OPPOSITE A view of the rugged Chiricahua Mountains in southeastern Arizona.

Jon looking for birds and beauty in the Chiricahuas.

fun is capturing our finds with his Nikon. Checks have appeared on my list for the bridled titmouse, painted redstart, yellow-eyed junco, magnificent hummingbird, lesser goldfinch, brown creeper, along with a note about hearing—but not seeing—the elusive, whiskered screech owl.

In our hunt for the elegant trogon, a large Christmas-colored tropical bird found seasonally in the high sycamore stands of the Chiricahuas, our visual search was, and has remained, futile. We studied the habits, behaviors and sounds of the bird and began listening as well as watching. I read a book about bird watching and learned never to wear white while in pursuit. When we tromped through areas of prime habitat, we learned to stop and be still, letting the forest return to an undisturbed silence. In this posture of quiet listening, we eventually were able to hear the distinctive croak of an elegant trogon, sounding very much like a sea lion. Although we have yet to see one, we know that nothing in the realm of bird watching can be hurried, and so we must be patient and will just keep returning.

On one foray in the Chiricahuas, we crossed a dry riverbed and stopped in mid-stride as we glanced to our right. Simultaneously we spotted a furtive creature that had also stopped in its tracks, sizing us up. An animal we had never seen before held us spellbound. My binoculars snapped to attention and Jon's camera clicked furiously as the shy stranger with a long ringed tail slunk away. We saw no new birds that day, but were enriched by our brief encounter with the elusive coatimundi.

Then, the year Cosme padded her way into our lives, we decided to drive up the west coast of California for a different kind of sighting, that of a tiny Crane. In recent years, as our children have had children, we have added a spur to our homeward journey, an emotional detour that takes us up the west coast from Los Angeles to Kennewick, Washington. Between the two cities, four little grandsons keep eating, thriving, learning amazing new words, and becoming a priority in our schedule.

But on this, Cosme's first American journey—before meeting the newest baby, before recording any new west-coast bird sightings—we stopped for a brief training mission: Civilizing the Free-Ranging Mexican Cat. Our base camp was Joshua Tree National Park. We decided that to have a traveling cat meant to have a cat on a leash, so we began training ours first by getting her used to a harness. She initially bucked at the harness, but we

On a bird-watching hike, we spotted the elusive coatimundi instead.

Cactus in bloom in Joshua Tree National Park.

thought we saw progress in a kind of resignation over a few days' time, and decided then to attach the leash.

By this time, Cosme already had a little experience with the concept of harness and leash, having stayed for a short time with our friends, Katy and Mel, in Baja. Two months earlier, we had left Baja to fly to South Dakota for Jon to receive an award from the Governor for distinction in creative achievement. We could not fly with a kitty, so we left the camper and its furry occupant with our friends at Los Frailes on Baja's east cape. She was so brand new to us that we had no idea how she would behave, but our friends were brave and took on the challenge. Being nervous that the cat would run away, Katy fashioned a harness out of heavy ribbon and tried to govern Cosme's movements. She told us the kitten kept slipping out of it, because she was so skinny. However, Katy did not tell us until years later what a bloody catastrophe that was. Scratched and bleeding from her efforts, she gave the job of pet oversight to Mel, who learned to corral Cosme by dangling a toy on a long stick to lead the wild thing in and out of the camper. They earned the status of aunt and uncle of the year.

Then it was our turn to enforce the leash. "Let's go for a walk, Cosme," Jon cajoled as he snapped the leash in place. She tugged, pulled away, braked, growled, and complained as he tried to drag her stiff-legged through the sandy desert. Eventually, she simply lay down, as if to say, "Drag me if you must, but I'll have no part of this." End of game. Cosme 1; Leash 0.

Thankfully, she must have had some misplaced dog genes in her DNA, because we discovered that she loved to go for walks with us untethered. We walked out into the desert without the leash, and she followed, talking to us the entire way. She stayed close, occasionally darting off our path to chase lizards, but never out of sight. Despite my best efforts to assert, "She's just a cat. I'm not going to worry about her or treat her like my baby," she wiggled her way under my skin in a manner that felt to me much like motherhood. Although I could never detach enough not to worry, I did learn about her penchant for staying close to her papa and her food bowl. On one of our early desert hikes, she came along until Jon turned around, needing to get back to his painting. I wanted to walk further. Cosme followed me for a bit, but as soon as Jon and the camper began to disappear from view, she swiveled and headed toward home.

Cosme also took to the American Southwest's canyon country, no doubt because of the endless supply of lizards. Or maybe it's because of the new color that enters her wardrobe when she rolls in the red dirt. As often as possible, our route home includes some portion of the canyon country of southern Utah and northern Arizona. The area is like an opulent, red magnet that draws us in like the love of a grandmother.

A friend told me once that she knew we had become cat people when we started choosing campsites based on what was best not only for us, but more importantly, for our traveling feline. In

OPPOSITE Cosme became an avid fan of bouldering in Joshua Tree.

Enticing canyon country of southern Utah.

the desert Southwest, we became aware of Cosme's vulnerability, especially to aggressive and predatory birds. At Marble Canyon near Lee's Ferry in Arizona, we found a remote campsite on a stone precipice overlooking the Colorado River as it flowed far below. For two days, we hiked along the rim in both directions, catching sight of numerous rafting expeditions on the way from Lee's Ferry through the Grand Canyon. The landscape offered no trees or bushes for a cat's protection, only unrelenting wind and vast, distant views. One day as she followed us out on the rim, a couple of very aggressive ravens dive-bombed her, sending her ducking for the cover of the camper, tail fluffed up, body low, and ears back. She knew not to venture far after that, and we left the next day in search of a friendlier cat environment.

We did not find it at House Rock Valley, a Vermillion Cliffs refuge and viewing station for the California condors. A reintroduction effort began here in 1996, creating an area for the birds to safely repopulate. The viewing station was at least a mile from the cliff where the condors soared, which was not close enough to see the birds well or get sharp photographs. I would have settled for that vantage point, but Jon never lets a little distance stand between him and a great shot. We left Cosme in the camper as we trekked across the red rocks toward the base of the cliffs. From that vantage point, we were able to see the patterns under their wings, gape at their orange-tinted, bald heads, and marvel at the expanse of their wings as they caught thermals in an upward spiral. I shook my head as we hiked back to the camper, filled with wonder once again, tucking away the memory of what I might have missed without Jon's insistent push past the good in favor of the best.

From there, we traveled further up along the Vermillion Cliffs to find a cozy, secluded campsite in the piñon juniper forest at around 6,000 feet in altitude. Jon's Facebook post described it as "miles from anyone, except maybe for the spirits of the 'Ancient Ones' who once lived in the archeological site on the cliffs above us." He scouted out the cliffs while Cosme and I stuck a little closer to the camper, tucking in after a chilly amble around the camp.

As I wrote the word "Facebook," I thought of how different our travels are now than when we were first married in 1993, at least in terms of communication. Most stories in this book came from my handwritten journals, not from an electronic memory bank. Before cell phones, we used pay phones. In Baja, that would

A cat's version of living on the edge.

mean leaving a remote beach once a week, driving into town, tracking down a place to buy a phone card, and searching for a phone booth on some noisy street corner. Every conversation would begin the same way. "We've got ten minutes. What's happening?" Now, regardless of which beach, canyon, valley, or desert we might visit—in either the United States, Mexico, or Canada—we can reach out at any time through the marvels of a mobile satellite connection. Our world has changed, and we enjoy the convenience, but resist the constant electronic attachment. An hour or two a day suits us just fine.

Another benefit of our mobile satellite has been the use of Google Earth. On our first sojourn through the Valley of the Gods in the far southeast corner of Utah, we drove the big loop through the valley and found a nice campsite that served as a good introduction to the area. We sauntered our way through astounding red rock formations and down dry creek beds splattered with a sage-colored mineral that looked like it had randomly spilled out of a giant paint bucket. On our second evening, Jon studied Google Earth. He was looking for a campsite that he suspected was hidden back the way we had come, one we could not see from the road. The next morning we went in search. Thanks to Jon's determination and the Google Earth app, we hit upon a secluded spot that was perfectly situated for hiking up an interesting canyon yet unknown to us. We stayed another couple of days, taking long hikes and memorizing the beauty of this enchanted valley.

Camping in the Valley of the Gods in southern Utah.

When we drove out of the Valley of the Gods north toward the Moki Dugway and Muley Point on Road 261, we kept feeling as if someone had made a mistake on the map or on the signs. We could see no evidence of a road that continued up from the base of the cliff where the Moki Dugway should be. The closer we got to the stone wall ahead, the more certain we were that we would simply hit a dead end. However, at the last possible moment, a road materialized off to the right, and we began ascending a series of switchbacks that rivaled the dreaded Agua Verde Road in Baja. We inched upward, eyes torn between the rugged road and the majestic view that began opening to the south.

At the top, we found a road leading out to Muley Point, where a sign read "Road Impassable When Wet." We both know what gumbo roads are and, with rain in the forecast, we determined to leave the next day. Jon's Facebook post from this campsite read:

"PHOTOGRAPHER'S DREAM—We awoke this morning on Muley Point on Cedar Mesa, north of Mexican Hat, Utah. The air was hazy, but from our viewpoint on this mesa we could see the San Juan River canyons, with Monument Valley and Black Mesa in the distance." We absorbed as much as we could in twenty-four hours on this expansive rock edge that bordered on forever and observed Cosme's tentative movements as she watched for the coyotes we all knew were around.

Between Natural Bridges National Monument and Blanding, Utah, we discovered a remarkable area known for archeological ruins. At the north end of Butler Wash, we hiked a trail out to Butler Wash Indian Ruins, which had cliff dwellings and kivas dating back 700 years. Hiking up the southern end of Butler Wash and the canyons of Combs Ridge, we explored Anasazi sites— Monarch Ruins, Cold Spring Ruins, and the Wolf-Man petroglyphs—where we found ancient corn cobs and pot shards that sent us reeling with a sense of antiquity we have rarely experienced. These are among the 100,000 archeological sites that make up the Bear's Ears National Monument, an area in danger of commercial exploration for oil, gas, and coal.

One of Jon's Facebook posts reveals feelings evoked by having feet on the ground within what remains of this ancient and mystical world. "*ALONE WITH THE SPIRITS—There was nobody else around, at least nobody I could see or touch. I spent a warm, still, and quiet evening in a nearby canyon as I poked*

Cosme watches for coyotes in the canyonlands.

And then she strolls the fence post, away from the noise of the Pacific Ocean.

through the Anasazi ruins called Cold Spring Cave. It was so quiet. I can't say that the ancient spirits were with me, but..."

Eventually our calendar began to squawk and to demand that we pay attention to our shrinking allotment of time. Important visits awaited, so we were off and on our way, leaving ancient spirits behind in favor of new ones: grandchildren. First, instead of driving into Los Angeles and trying to camp on a city street, we arranged someplace on the periphery to gather with my son, Michael, his wife, Allison, and our grandson, Miller. Ojai, Joshua Tree, and La Jolla have become favorite places to share a few special days and to watch young Miller engage with nature—and our onboard entertainer, Cosme.

And as the seasons have passed, Cosme has continued to make the rules. When we are off the beaten track, she patrols the perimeter of the campsite and stays close to the camper. We don't even bother to stop at US campgrounds with rules that require all pets to be leashed, because she has explained clearly—in two languages—that she will have none of it. And so, in cities, areas with busy streets, or neighborhoods with off-leash dogs, she nests indoors. Cosme 1: Civilization (disqualified).

Leaving Los Angeles and heading north to Washington one year, we camped along California's Highway 1 south of Big Sur, across the highway from the ocean access. We thought since she was a Baja cat, Cosme would love to romp on the beach, so we toted her across the highway in her carrier, descended a long flight

of wooden stairs to the shore, and opened the carrier for her to run free. To our astonishment, she seemed terrified and began running desperately away from the water, ears back and eyes wide. She was like a trapped fugitive, escaping toward the wall of rock and vegetation abutting the water's edge. We finally caught up with her, got her back into the carrier, and hauled her up to the top of the stairs, where we calmed her down and enjoyed the view. We also considered Cosme's reaction, eventually guessing that the sound of the ocean had reverberated off the rock wall so intensely that her sensitive feline ears just could not make sense of it. The Baja beach on the calm Sea of Cortez had not prepared her for the thunder of the Pacific.

Neither had our calm Baja beach prepared Cosme for the thunder of three little boys in Kennewick, where our travels take us to visit Jon's son, Adam, wife Chelsea, and our grandsons, Calvin, Farley, and Dylan. Our time there is dizzying, exhausting, and precious, and it always ends too soon.

Another year after our family visits along the west coast, we headed east through Washington, camping the first night along the Snake River. When we found our campsite in mid-afternoon, we heard a great-horned owl hooting and, with a curious cat at our side, wandered over to get pictures. Later, as the sun got lower, we watched the sunset, with Cosme playing in front of us. Suddenly, she bolted upright, jerked around, and clawed her way up a tree. Within seconds, the owl appeared, perching in the tree above her, joined

OPPOSITE Grandson Miller and Cosme become acquainted in La Jolla, California. (Photo by Gail Crane, March 2018.)

Our Kennewick, Washington, grandsons—from left: Farley, Dylan, and Calvin. (Photo by Chelsea Crane, July 2019.)

shortly by a second owl. Several times, Jon and I shooed the birds away, and tried to coax our wary kitten down to take her inside, but she clung fiercely to her refuge in the tree, refusing to budge.

My fear for our furball got the best of me when one owl spread his wings ominously over her tree and the other one began making a clattering sound that we could not interpret. Were they trying to tell her to stay away from their hunting grounds—or were they telling her she was about to be dinner? As we chased the owls away once again, Jon grabbed a step stool and was finally able to sweet-talk her down, close enough to grab one paw and pull her into his arms. We scurried with her into the camper, where she promptly curled up in our bed, quite nonchalant, as if to say, "*¿Quién necesita una correa*?" (Who needs a leash?) Cosme 1: Owls 0.

The next night we traveled as far as Columbus, Montana, and began looking for a place to stop for the night. Jon did his usual thing, driving past the easy-to-find places I pointed out, like the city park, out into the countryside and up the river to a fishing access with a compelling view and few folks around. Cosme had plenty of room to roam safely, until a wild turkey sent her ducking for cover, but that scuffle seemed playful compared to the owl encounter of the night before.

Many of our heading-home stories involve Montana and Wyoming, two neighboring states through which we travel when coming from the West Coast. I remember arriving late in the day at the Lower Lake of Red Rock Lakes National Wildlife Area on

The great-horned owl in pursuit of Cosme.

Cosme refusing to budge from her tree refuge.

the southern edge of Montana as we headed east. Clouds were approaching from the south and east, with a good chance of severe thunderstorms in the forecast. In the cab of the truck, we waited out one brief squall, studying the brochure of the refuge. As the rain tapered off, we opened the camper and started supper. Clouds to the south remained dark and threatening, moving our way. Within a few minutes, the camper was slammed with a violent gust of wind, sending Cosme into a panic and Jon to the back door to peer out. As he let out an incredulous "Oh, wow!" I slid out the door behind him, holding onto the railing with a grip that echoed Jon's exclamation. Sun had pierced the clouds, spotlighting in gold the field of grass that undulated wildly under the powerful force of the wind.

We looked south toward the mountains, where a rainbow glowed with the same fierce intensity of the struggling gold-lit grass. The wind became fiercer, and the colors of the rainbow deepened, as if to up the ante. Camera in hand, Jon ventured down the stairs, trying to do his photographer's job of documenting the beauty, only to be blown off his feet onto the ground several times. He could not hear me yelling to him, voice trembling, over the force of the gale. Barely breathing, I remembered Jon's admonition not to be afraid of the forces of nature, but rather to take energy from them. As I absorbed the power, violence, intensity, and beauty tangled all together around us, a second rainbow appeared, as if to bring strength to the first and to us. My prayers became praises as we stood together in the wake, watching the storm move on into the

Double rainbow during a storm at Red Rock Lakes National Wildlife Refuge.

bleeding colors of sunset. Writing this memory, I find myself lost in a song expressive of my response to God's presence that day:

You are my hiding place
You always fill my heart
With songs of deliverance
Whenever I am afraid.
I will trust in You
I will trust in You
Let the weak say "I am strong
*In the strength of the Lord."**

* From words written by Michael James Ledner, based on Psalm 32:7

We are almost home now as we drive through the Bighorn Mountains of Wyoming, flashing back through hundreds of memories of camping along her rivers and streams amid the pine trees and willows. In these mountains, I learned the thrill of trout fishing in small streams and the exhaustion from catching so many fish that you cannot fling the fly one more time. I eventually came to terms with my aversion to ripping a hook out of fish lips to let them go, and instead discovered the charm of simply hiking along with my husband as he fished, poetry in motion. I felt his tangible release from the pressures of life as he studied the stream, matched the hatch, and dropped the fly in precisely the right pool. I learned to hike far out of the way to keep from getting between the mama moose and her young, and I learned just how cold Freeze-Out Point could be.

With Cosme on board one year, I learned to always lock the back door to the camper as we traveled. Once, in a hurry to get to a new and very promising fishing hole high in the Bighorns, we closed, but did not bother to lock, the camper door. Ten miles up into the mountains on a gravel road, we found our destination and got ready to hit the stream. We walked around to the back of the camper and discovered the door wide open. Terrified, we peered through the door, wondering if we still had a cat. To our great relief, Cosme tiptoed out through the thick dust, sneezing and meowing as if to say, "Why didn't you lock the door? *Qué tontos.*" (What sillies.)

Jon fishing a small stream in the Bighorn Mountains of Wyoming. (Photo by Gail Crane, 2018.)

I recall once driving home from an out-of-the-way campsite on the Middle Fork of the Powder River. Jon asked me to drive Ruby, our tow car, for about twenty-two miles to make it easier for him to negotiate the ruts in the dirt road. The weather was good, a beautiful day for traveling, and as I drove, I began to sing the Lord's Prayer. I sang it over and over with a seeking heart. The road led up a steep hill, and as Ruby crested the top, my amen collided with a stunning view across a red rock canyon that opened below me. The last notes of my love song caught in my throat and mingled with the tears that always come when I feel God is near. I am so often blinded to this beauty by my busy-ness. This day, He made sure I did not miss Him in this wild and natural world, and gratitude was my guide as we made our way toward home.

images of mystic

FULL CIRCLE

chapter fourteen

As the camper dips and sways off the gravel county road, levels out and heads into our valley, Jon and I feel the familiar anticipation of coming to the end of the long road home. We breathe in the scent of pine and spruce, watch for patches of ice that might be lingering on this spring day, and grin with gratitude as we reach the driveway. Perhaps I should say I grin with gratitude, because Jon is never truly ready to leave the traveling adventures behind. To be fair, his jaw is set firmly as he thinks of the work that awaits him.

After what feels like a lifetime of traveling in tandem, we have fine-tuned our roles for the return, like the flight crews of an aircraft upon landing. As a flight attendant, I open doors, clean the inside of the camper, and put maps and books away. I lug in the laundry, restock the food supplies, and find homes for the rocks and shells that have crept into hiding places in the rig. Time on the road means a pile of phone messages blinking on the answering machine, and that is my job, too.

Our furry companion, Cosme, gingerly steps down from the camper, nose sniffing and ears twitching, and she begins her familiar rounds. Her main job, after rolling in the dirt, is to take an inventory of the rodent population, no doubt making a schedule of which garden to attend to first. She tracks the movements of her food and water bowls to be sure they are properly restored to their former location in the house. She also assists with the emotional well-being of the flight crew, making us laugh and lighten up with

Cosme becoming reacquainted with the neighborhood after a long winter away.

Sometimes our arrival home in May is a chilly landing.

her antics as she sniffs through dead flies and cobwebs or tears across the living room hoping for a game of chase.

The reason Jon's jaw is clenched and his brow is furrowed is that his jobs are the most complex, starting with the landing itself. As the pilot and ground crew, he begins by detaching the tow car, emptying the holding tanks and rolling the camper into the correct position with a southern exposure for good satellite reception—because it remains our source of electronic contact all year. Just as in our early days, Jon coaxes the water to flow in the house, places strategic fires to warm the corners and the bed, and re-establishes the Internet connection. In my estimation, he is somewhat of a magician, especially when Mystic is still covered in snow.

As I watch him grapple with the nitty-gritty aspects of bringing water, warmth, and technology to this little patch of earth, and as he muses about which new project he will tackle now that we have landed home, my heart melts. I watch his gaze as he contemplates the property with plans bubbling up that nobody else can imagine, and I reflect on the words of our sometimes-traveling companion, Paula.

"Jon has that rare quality of being a man who believes in himself. I think people are drawn to him, in part, because of that thing in him that makes a blank canvas something he thinks he can fill. He has spent his whole life deciding how to fill blank spaces with his unique vision of what they could or should contain. And then, of course, he is determined and ornery enough to make the

Walking through a familiar tunnel on the Mickelson Trail—the one dedicated to Jon.

The trestle that spans Castle Creek in the Mystic Valley.

vision happen, every day, on one hand with color and light and line, and on another with building materials or friends or activity. That is what I think is so remarkable, what draws us like moths to a bright light. The rest of us just want to get up close to that and figure out the magic."

As I put on my well-worn hiking boots and amble through the valley we call home, past placer mines, through a tunnel, and over trestles, I ponder the ups and downs of my journey with this determined, ornery Mystic traveler of mine, this man who so fully believes in himself. The memories reverberate in my mind. Climbing the mountain across the creek from our home, I feel safe if my feet land directly in Jon's footprints. I can cross the creek on a log as long as he is in front of me, beckoning me forward. On many desert hikes, his scarred, leather backpack has made me smile with assurance as I amble behind him. Kayaking in Baja is less frightening if I can see him ahead of me as we paddle, and I need him to land first so he can pull my kayak through the waves to shore. With each step or stroke, I learn to trust, and the more I can trust him the more I find myself trusting beyond this human realm. The words on that gold band on my finger, "Whither thou goes, I will go," have become a mantra, not only for my human love relationship, but also for my relationship with the Source of all life and love. The circle widens, claims me, assures me, and leads me in God's grace to the next adventure.

I would follow this man's backpack anywhere.

Photos have captured the places we've been, and sifting through this deep reservoir of images lures me back to what we have seen and tasted and smelled and touched. But some of the sights from the edge are more like an inner knowing—insights born of encounters, relationships, or presence.

Thinking about the changes to my inner landscape, I catch a glimpse of a vast area where a bulldozer has been at work. Jagged outcroppings of fear have been smoothed down and replaced, leaving gardens of acceptance, curiosity, and respect. This inner change is an understanding of the interconnectedness of all life on the planet. As a long-time explorer of wilderness, I'm sure Jon received this gift long before I did. But I had to be led, tiptoeing along the line between the known and the unknown, learning how earthworms work in my garden, gasping at the size of the whale shark in the sea, or discerning the sound of a quail call in the desert. With each step, I began to feel a tug to get closer, to understand, to shake hands, and to memorize the face of the new member of my world. "Out there" somehow became not an edge, but a center, a family reunion.

Joseph Wood Krutch, in *Man's Ancient Powerful Link to Nature*, put it this way:

"On some summer vacation or some country weekend we realize that what we are experiencing is more than merely a relief from the pressures of city life; that we have not merely escaped from something but also INTO something; that we have joined the

Cosme studies a new member of her world.

I'm hungry to know more about the birds I see.

greatest of all communities, which is not that of men alone but of everything that shares with us the great adventure of being alive."

Recently Jon held a spotlight on another plot of reworked earth in my heart. He confided his new mantra, one he recites each morning as he embraces the innocent newness of the dawn. "I am grateful for this day." He even learned it and often says it in Spanish: "*Estoy agradecido por este dia.*" Given all our diverging approaches to life's complexities, this has become a community garden we work together. Over many years, I've come to realize that planting the seeds of gratitude helps to choke out the noxious weeds of negativity, anxiety, fear, and doubt.

The Mystic Travelers Corps of Exploration has stopped to light many candles in roadside shrines along the narrow and unsettling roads of Baja. We offer up prayers for traveling mercies as well as prayers of thanksgiving, leaning into the mystery of the Divine presence with us. Being grateful in spite of the potholes makes it easier to anticipate the sunset at the end of the long day's drive. Saying thank you when the hiking trail takes me huffing and puffing straight up the mountain helps me to acknowledge that my heart will be healthier for the strain. Finding gratitude in the face of the wind is a whole different story, but I try to pretend to be experimenting with a new tousled look for my hair. This approach is still a work in progress. But I work hard at tending this part of my inner landscape, because it makes my world a happier place to be.

I can think of one other transformation that wandering along the edge has created inside my soul. I'm hungry all the time. I am writing these words in a secluded place in southeastern Arizona, near Aravaipa Canyon. Yesterday we hiked up a wash and through a slot in the cliff that took us to the other side of the mountain. We saw several birds we were not able to identify for sure. I'm hungry to know who they were. The day before, we drove a narrow, rutted trail along a ridge to an overlook of what might be Turkey Creek Canyon far below. Does the road go there? I'm hungry to know. Gorging on nature seems to feed my desire to have more.

Jon always says that his favorite painting is the next one. We might agree on this as a philosophy for travel as well. As we journey farther up the trail, we will continue searching for the next favorite sight, or insight, as we explore beyond the known. Pressing toward the edge, we will gather the mysteries that make us whole.

OPPOSITE Go to *mystictravelers.us* to browse a more complete library of travel photos by Jon Crane.

images of mystic

ACKNOWLEDGMENTS

I am grateful to live close to the small town of Hill City, South Dakota, where the arts are highly valued and nurtured. The Hill City Arts Council sponsored writers' workshops that connected me with two skilled and supportive mentors—Pamela Smith Hill, who caught my vision and encouraged me to go forth and write, and local author Linda Hasselstrom, who pushed, polished, and empowered me until the manuscript was completed.

Kathryn Cleveland, Jan Johnson, and Ron Walker came from Hill City's writing community to listen and fine-tune my thoughts. Linda Flounders sent an angel my way in the person of Pam Ramsey, whose relentless eye for detail and literary expertise became invaluable.

For information about Mystic's history, I turned to those who knew or had lived the stories, and I was enriched by their insights—Margaret Brown Anderson, Jim and Carolyn Brown, Linda Dolan, Joyce Glover Dryden, Russel and Pam Frink (following Russel's death, Pam remarried, becoming Pam Kaubisch), Jay Hendrickson, Paula Jones, Lorraine Rye, Linda Sandness, and Roy Schiefer. Baja stories were informed by John Boutwell, Jerry and Pat Harvey, and Gary Steele, while our beach musicians Don Carlon and Steve Smith generously shared their songs. Then there is Paula Efta, a.k.a. Elmerita, who spanned the space between Mystic and Baja with her words, becoming our Elmer's glue once again.

My love forever to my husband Jon Crane for being my intrepid guide.

Hill City's own Kristin Donnan took this embryo under her wing, kept it warm and safe, then held it up by its heels, spanked it, and brought it into the world. I offer my deepest gratitude to John Edwards for consulting on the design, and to Rockin' Dog Studio for believing in the project and being my champion.

Many mornings as I sat down to write, I would pray these lines from an 18th century hymn:

Come Thou Fount of every blessing,
Tune my heart to sing Thy grace.

Here, then, I add my heartfelt gratitude to God for His faithful guidance, with the hope that my words would be a pleasing love song to the One who gave me the desire to sing of His grace.

ABOUT THE AUTHOR

Gail McNary Crane was raised in Texas. There, she attended the University of Texas in Austin, earning a Bachelor's Degree in Education with a double minor in English and Spanish. In her first marriage, which ended in 1985, she had two children, Amanda and Michael. She was a secondary Spanish and English teacher for several years in Arlington, Texas.

After meeting Jon Crane at an art show in Dallas, the couple married in 1993, and they have lived in South Dakota since 1994. She is the director of Jon Crane Watercolors, Inc., where she assists her husband in the publishing, promotion, and distribution of his art. Jon and Gail share a love for nature's tranquility, as well as its challenges. They enjoy gardening, fly-fishing, kayaking, hiking, and searching for out-of-the-way places that will provide inspiration for Jon's next watercolor painting. They reside near Mystic, South Dakota, with Cosme, the cat who adopted them in Baja, Mexico.